THE
Chia Seed Cookbook

Skyhorse Publishing books may be purchased in bulk at special discounts for sales promotion, corporate gifts, fund-raising, or educational purposes. Special editions can also be created to specifications. For details, contact the Special Sales Department, Skyhorse Publishing, 307 West 36th Street, 11th Floor, New York, NY 10018 or info@skyhorsepublishing.com.

Skyhorse® and Skyhorse Publishing® are registered trademarks of Skyhorse Publishing, Inc.®, a Delaware corporation.

Visit our website at www.skyhorsepublishing.com.

10 9 8 7 6 5 4 3 2 1

Library of Congress Cataloging-in-Publication Data is available on file.

ISBN:978-1-62087-427-1

Printed in China

Eat Well, Feel Great, Lose Weight

THE
Chia Seed Cookbook

MYSEEDS CHIA TEST KITCHEN

SKYHORSE PUBLISHING

Table *of* Contents

INTRODUCTION

Y ou may have heard of chia seeds, but do you know just how good they are for you, and how versatile they are?

The chia plant is a relative of the mint plant. It makes tiny, flavorless seeds in either white or dark brown. (Though the colors range into gray, black, tan, and off-white—every chia seed has a different pattern on the shell.) The different seed colors have slightly different nutritional properties. For instance, the black seed has slightly more fiber, while the white seed has slightly more protein. The black seed also has a higher concentration of the anti-oxidant Anthocyanin, which helps prevent free radical damage and signs of premature aging. Anthocyanin is the plant pigment that gives dark colored foods their hue. For optimal nutrition, MySeeds always mixes together black and white chia.

The chia plant produces an oil in the stems and leaves that insects and other pests can't stand. When the plant itself is safely and naturally repelling pests, there's no need to use pesticides. Since chia grows in hot, sandy, dry, and poor soil, it doesn't compete with other crops. These factors contribute to making chia easy to grow in an all-natural way.

Unlike almost all other foods, chia has no flavor of its own. When raw, it tastes like nothing at all. This means you can't hate it, but it can get boring since there's no flavor. Fortunately, chia does not dilute or replace flavors when you add it to foods you already like to eat. Instead, it will distribute the flavor, or even take on the taste of the food it's in. For example, if you add chia to chocolate pudding, then it will be chocolaty. Add it to strawberry yogurt? Then it will taste strawberry.

This introduction will help you understand chia so you know exactly how to use it to get the results you're looking for.

Chia Gel

Throughout the book, you'll see chia gel as an ingredient. Chia gel forms when the chia seed is exposed to water or non-acidic liquids. The soluble fiber on the outside of the seed shell hydrates and forms a bead of gelatin around the seed. You'll see chia gel used in several ways throughout the book. It can be used to substitute butter or oil, it can help combine flavors together, and it can function as a flavor-extender for things like salad dressings.

Chia gel is also super easy to make with this simple ratio: "9 to 1." That's 9 parts water to 1 part chia.

1 tablespoon dry chia seeds
9 tablespoons filtered water

Put your chia seeds and water in a resealable container, shake or stir to prevent clumping . . . and in about 15 minutes you'll have chia gel! The gel will keep for about a week in the fridge in a covered container. (If uncovered, it will dry up.) Every tablespoon of dry chia goes far in the kitchen, so it's a great value too.

Why "filtered water"?

Chia gel is not supposed to taste like anything; however, the gelling action can sometimes magnify flavors. If there were any unsavory flavors in the tap water, they could be more pronounced in the gel, so for best taste, it's important to use pure water.

It's this amazing gelling ability that makes your digestive system treat ordinary water as it would food. The stomach has to strip the soluble fiber away to access the water. This means the gelled seeds stay in the stomach longer, to help it continue sending "I'm full" signals to the brain.

Chia can help you with so many goals—from losing weight by keeping you feeling full longer, to providing steady energy with its high protein content, to kick-starting your recipes with extra nutrition while cutting out fat. But how can just one tiny seed do all of this? Check out the top ten ways that chia can help your health.

1.   Lose Weight Without Starving

The Chia Seed is a dieter's dream come true. The tiny, healthy seeds can be made to taste like whatever you want, and their unique gelling action keeps you feeling full for hours. Hunger is a main enemy of real weight loss, and you don't want to fight it with jitter-inducing, expensive pills. When a chia seed is exposed to water, it forms a coating of gel, increasing its size and weight. Since the gel is made of water, it has no calories. It's also difficult to remove the water from the seed, meaning that it helps your body think it is full without adding calories!

2.   Balance Blood Sugar

Keeping balanced levels of blood sugar is important for both health and energy. Blood sugar may spike after meals, especially if you eat high-starchy foods or sweets. This can lead to "slumps" in your day where you feel tired and out of energy. By balancing your blood sugar, you not only lower your risk for type-2 diabetes, but also ensure steady, constant energy throughout your day.

How does the Chia Seed help with this? Both the gelling action of the seed and its unique combination of soluble and insoluble fiber combine to slow down your body's conversion of starches into sugars. If you eat chia with a meal, it will help you turn your food into constant, steady energy rather than a series of ups and downs that wear you out.

3.   Help Prevent Diverticulitis / Diverticulosis

With the abundance of over-processed foods and white flour on the market today, rich sources of fiber are harder to come by. These foods of convenience have contributed to the rise of diverticulitis. Irregularity is a big factor in this risky condition. To help ensure regularity, you need plenty of soluble and insoluble fiber in your diet. If you don't want to eat celery and whole-grain everything—or piles of bran flakes—the chia seed is here to help. Each seed is coated with soluble fibers that aid its gelling action. The exterior of the seed is protected by insoluble fiber. Because the stomach cannot break down or digest the insoluble fiber, the chia seed helps keep food moving smoothly through the digestive process and does not contribute any calories. Soluble fiber and the gel coating of the seed keep the colon hydrated and ensure the easy movement of food.

4.   Add healthy omega-3 oil to your diet

Omega-3 oil is usually thought of as "that healthy stuff in fish." But what if you don't want to eat fish every day? What if you're a vegetarian or simply worried about pollution adding harmful substances to your fish dinner? Chia is the richest plant-source of this healthy oil. By weight, chia contains more omega 3 than salmon, and it still tastes like whatever you want! Omega 3 oil is important in heart and cholesterol health. It's also recently been targeted as a weight-loss helper. USA Weekend magazine also reported that overweight dieters who included omega 3s in their eating plan lost two more pounds monthly than the control group who did not.

5.   Feel more energized all day long

Don't want to feel like taking an afternoon nap? Your energy levels have a lot to do with what you eat. Chia is one of nature's highest plant-based sources of complete protein.

Usually protein from items like peanut butter and some beans are incomplete, meaning you have to combine them with other foods to get the full benefit. Not chia, though—its protein is complete and will raise your energy levels. The combination of complete protein, vitamins, minerals, and blood-sugar balancing gel all work together to make sure you have steady, never jittery energy.

6.   Bake with less fat

Do you enjoy making baked goods at home, but hate all the butter and oil that has to go into them? Chia gel can substitute for half the butter in most recipes! The food will bake the same and taste the same (or better) from the addition of the chia gel. All you need to do is divide the amount of butter or oil in about half, and then use the same amount of chia gel to fill in. The anti-oxidants in chia can even help keep the food tasting fresh longer. Cookies, cakes, muffins, pancakes, dessert bars, and more can be made with chia gel as your butter replacement. Which recipe will become your new favorite?

7.   Add age-defying anti-oxidants

Anti-oxidants are often in the news for their super health benefits. You know that blueberries and several exotic fruits (that aren't always in season) have them, but did you know that chia is extremely high in anti-oxidants too? These helpful substances are what make the chia seed stay fresh for so long. At room temperature, they'll stay fresh and ready to eat for more than two whole years! And that's all without a single chemical or preservative. This amazing ability is not found in other seeds like flax or sesame; those seeds don't have the same rich anti-oxidant content.

Anti-oxidants help prevent free-radical damage in your body. Free radicals lead to problematic conditions such as premature aging of the skin and inflammation of various tissues. Fight free radical damage by staying fresh and healthy with nature's anti-oxidant powerhouse.

8.   Cut cravings for food

A deficiency in minerals or vitamins can create a craving for food. For example, if you're low on calcium, you may feel compelled to eat lots of cheese and ice cream. This happens because your body knows that cheese is a source of calcium, and it hasn't been getting enough. But what if dairy and whole milk are a "diet don't"? You can always add calcium to your food by sprinkling on the chia. By weight, chia has more calcium than whole milk. It also has magnesium and boron, essential trace minerals used in the absorption of calcium and other vitamins. By balancing your vitamins and minerals with chia, you can curb cravings that might tempt you.

9.   You can pack in a more flavorful punch

How can a seed with NO flavor help the foods you already like taste better? First, because they have no taste of their own, chia seeds will never mask or overpower the flavor of your food. Second, when the seeds hydrate, they magnify the taste of whatever they were added to. Put them in pudding? Chocolaty! Swirl them into a smoothie? Fruity! The same thing goes with dressings, dips, salsas, sauces, and more. These two factors combine to let chia seeds take on the taste of whatever you add them to. They distribute and never dilute the flavors you love.

10.   Save your money

Why should eating less cost you more? You already know diet pills are expensive, and "box meal plans" can run up to $500 a month. If you're buying "calorie counting packs" or other individual portions in the store, you end up paying extra for all the preparation and materials that go into each package. More than enough chia for one month costs less than a dollar a day. You can use as much or as little as you want to achieve your desired results. There are no preparations required for these simple seeds; pesticides are not even required to grow them. They're always safe and 100 percent chemical free. A measuring spoon is all you'll need when you're ready to take advantage of chia for yourself. It doesn't get any easier or inexpensive.

Want to know more about specific issues that chia can help? Curious about more of the science with chia? You can visit us at www.mychiaseeds.com for a collection of interesting chia seed articles, videos, and more.

Now that you have your chia seeds, the question becomes: "What am I supposed to do with them?"

We have assembled healthy, tasty, alternative choices that you can add to your family's menus. Since you can make chia taste like anything you want, it's great for picky eaters. Add fiber and nutrients to kids' favorite snacks or even introduce them to a new one! (Just wait until you see the fun chia popsicles!)

Everyone knows that incorporating more fruits and veggies into a daily meal plan will really boost your immune system and will give you steady energy. We want you to know how to do this easily and deliciously. We want you to know exactly what is in your food. No additives, no grease, no high fructose corn syrup! By adding the amazing power of chia you can super charge your body and feel full faster and longer.

The MySeeds test kitchen is composed of cooks like you, not fancy chefs. All of the recipes are meant to be easy to prepare for anyone, use ingredients available in almost any grocery, and require only simple cookware. Discover the excitement of delicious healthy food and all of its benefits with these easy-to-prepare and highly nutritious recipes.

Enjoy!

METRIC AND IMPERIAL CONVERSIONS
(These conversions are rounded for convenience)

Ingredient	Cups/Tablespoons/ Teaspoons	Ounces	Grams/Milliliters
Butter	1 cup=16 tablespoons= 2 sticks	8 ounces	230 grams
Cream cheese	1 tablespoon	0.5 ounce	14.5 grams
Cheese, shredded	1 cup	4 ounces	110 grams
Chia seeds, dry	1 tablespoon	0.32 ounce	9 grams
Cornstarch	1 tablespoon	0.3 ounce	8 grams
Flour, all-purpose	1 cup/1 tablespoon	4.5 ounces/0.3 ounce	125 grams/8 grams
Flour, whole wheat	1 cup	4 ounces	120 grams
Fruit, dried	1 cup	4 ounces	120 grams
Fruits or veggies, chopped	1 cup	5 to 7 ounces	145 to 200 grams
Fruits or veggies, pureed	1 cup	8.5 ounces	245 grams
Honey, maple syrup, or corn syrup	1 tablespoon	.75 ounce	20 grams
Liquids: cream, milk, water, or juice	1 cup	8 fluid ounces	240 milliliters
Oats	1 cup	5.5 ounces	150 grams
Salt	1 teaspoon	0.2 ounces	6 grams
Spices: cinnamon, cloves, ginger, or nutmeg (ground)	1 teaspoon	0.2 ounce	5 milliliters
Sugar, brown, firmly packed	1 cup	7 ounces	200 grams
Sugar, white	1 cup/1 tablespoon	7 ounces/0.5 ounce	200 grams/12.5 grams
Vanilla extract	1 teaspoon	0.2 ounce	4 grams

Chia Seed

Breakfasts

In today's busy world, many people underestimate the power of breakfast. It's the easiest meal of the day to skip since hunger usually isn't that intense in the morning, and there are always plenty of excuses: not enough time; or all the fast breakfasts are fast food; or the "good for you stuff" tastes bad.

However, breakfast plays an important role throughout your day. If you skip breakfast, you're very likely to want to snack before lunch or feel tired later on in the morning as your energy runs down. Caffeine is not a substitute for nutrition, no matter how many people treat it that way. Missing breakfast can also lead to overeating at lunch time or craving unhealthy foods. Having a healthy breakfast can help prevent blood sugar peaks and valleys that affect your energy level and concentration.

Breakfast foods are a great way to work healthy items into your day. You can use breakfast to boost your fiber, power up with protein, and have a serving or two of colorful fruits. These chia breakfasts can help you do all of the above. Most of the breakfasts you'll see are quick and easy. You can even prepare some ahead of time (like the banana breakfast pops) and keep them in the freezer. The breakfast oat squares can be made on a Sunday so you can simply pick one up as you head out the door Monday morning. It doesn't get much faster than that!

Whether they're a quick grab 'n' go (like the breakfast cookie) or suited for a fun Saturday morning (like the fruit crumple) you'll always be getting the added benefits of chia, without the preservatives or high fructose corn syrup of many packaged breakfast foods. When you have chia for breakfast, the two kinds of fiber in each seed will help ensure you stay full until to lunch time. The protein will provide you with energy to start your day off right.

A study from Virginia Commonwealth University found that regularly skipping breakfast increases your risk of significant weight gain by 450 percent! People who ate a protein-rich varied breakfast of about 400 calories lost more weight and kept it off because they had an easier time staying with their healthy life diet. Your mom was right! Breakfast gets your motor running.

Super Simple Ways to Add Chia to Your Breakfast

Breakfast could be the easiest meal of the day in which to use chia. These ideas are so simple that a recipe isn't even required. However, just because they're as easy as scoop-and-stir doesn't mean they should be overlooked.

- Stir dry chia into any flavor of yogurt—the seeds will take on the flavor of the yogurt.

- Stir chia gel into any type of oatmeal after cooking—you won't even notice the chia.

- Sprinkle chia over cereal if you plan to drink the milk afterward—some of the seeds will end up in the milk.

- Add chia gel to your breakfast tea—it will absorb the flavor of the tea and keep you feeling full.

- Toast with jam? Dry chia will stick in the jam.

- Making an omelet? Sprinkle dry chia before you fold it so it will stick in the egg.

- Add gelled chia to any breakfast drink to make it more filling.

- Swirling up a smoothie, protein shake, or anything else in the blender? Chia is ideal here, too.

- Healthy breakfast nut-butter sandwich! Sprinkle dry chia and top with banana slices. You can use peanut or almond butter for a change of pace.

Yogurt Berry Chia Parfaits

This isn't a recipe because it is just too easy. Ingredients: berries of choice, chia gel, and Greek yogurt. You can even prepare your parfaits the night before so they'll be ready to grab 'n' go in the morning. You may be the envy of your co-workers with such a beautiful breakfast or afternoon snack!

Like some crunch? You can add nuts such as cashews (shown on page 16) or almonds. Any nut that you like will work well here. When you're ready to eat, you can also sprinkle on a little granola so it doesn't become soggy. You can add as much or as little chia as you want to these parfaits . . . just use the amount that will keep you feeling full.

Chia and eggs are a great pair in the morning. Eggs provide protein, while chia provides fiber. With these quick recipes, you can see just how simple it is to add chia to eggs, however you like to prepare them.

Easy Chia Eggs

DIRECTIONS:

Melt the butter by microwaving it on high in a mug or small bowl for 30 seconds. Crack the egg into the melted butter and add the milk and the chia gel. With a fork, beat the eggs until scrambled.

Microwave the eggs on high power for 30 seconds. Stir. Microwave for another 30 seconds. The eggs will still be a little wet. Let the eggs set for about 2 minutes to finish cooking.

1 egg
½ tablespoon butter
1 tablespoon milk (cows, almond, rice etc.)
1 teaspoon chia gel

Easy does it omelet

DIRECTIONS:

In a small bowl, beat the eggs and milk. Melt the butter in a small skillet. Add egg mixture and cook over medium heat. As the eggs begin to set, lift the edges of the egg mixture so that the uncooked portion flows underneath. When the eggs are completely set, remove from heat. Place your choice of ingredients over half of the eggs, sprinkle with the chia, and fold the "top" over.

2 eggs

1 tablespoon milk (cows, almond, or rice)

1 teaspoon butter

1 teaspoon dry chia

Seasonings of your choice: basil, dill, red pepper flakes, etc.

Choose 2–3 omelet ingredients from the list:

sliced mushrooms,

diced onions,

torn spinach leaves,

diced red/green peppers,

diced tomatoes,

green apple slices,

thin sliced deli cheeses/meats.

{

Don't be afraid of the egg!

Eggs have gotten a lot of bad press in the past due to their cholesterol content. However, eggs are an excellent nutrient-dense food with six grams of protein, a bit of vitamin B-12, vitamin E, riboflavin, folic acid, calcium, zinc, iron, and essential fatty acids. An egg has just 75 calories. New insights into the fatty foods/heart disease connection reveal that in people with normal cholesterol metabolism, it is not cholesterol that clogs arteries; it is foods high in saturated and hydrogenated fats.

}

Cookies for breakfast? Who wouldn't get excited about that? These tasty, fruity, and filling cookies can provide you with an easy start to your day, even if you're in a rush. No time to have breakfast? Grab a cookie or two and away you go.

You can make a batch of these cookies on the weekend, and then grab one on the way out the door all week or pack them in a lunch bag. These breakfast cookies are loaded with fiber, protein, cinnamon, and fruit. If you let on about how healthy they are, will they still taste as good? Yes! This recipe makes about a dozen large cookies.

Breakfast Cookies!

DIRECTIONS:

In a medium mixing bowl, cream together the softened butter with the brown sugar, applesauce, and vanilla. Beat in the egg and then stir in the chia gel.

In a small mixing bowl, place the flours, baking soda, cinnamon, nutmeg, and oats. Stir to combine.

Add the dry ingredients to the wet ingredients and then stir in the flakes and dried fruits. These are to be large cookies so use about 3+ tablespoons of batter for each cookie. Press down lightly to flatten so that each cookie is about 3' round.

Bake on a cooking sprayed cookie sheet for about 11–12 minutes at 350 degrees. After the cookies have cooled, place in an air tight container.

¾ cup unbleached cake flour
½ cup all purpose flour
½ teaspoon baking soda
1½ teaspoon cinnamon
½ teaspoon nutmeg
½ cup quick cooking oats
½ cup of lightly smashed bran flakes dry cereal
¼ cup packed brown sugar
½ cup raisins OR
½ cup dried cranberries

Wet ingredients
¼ cup almond nut butter OR natural chunky peanut butter
¼ cup chia gel
4 oz. of applesauce
1 teaspoon vanilla
1 egg

Tip:

Why use cake flour in these cookies?
With oats, bran flakes, and nut butter, the batter can become "heavy" in texture. To make the cookies lighter and puffier, it's important to use cake flour, which doesn't have as much gluten.

Impress yourself with this Sunday French toast! Colorful fruits like strawberries, blueberries, or raspberries make a delicious topper for this toast. With a hint of citrus and Greek yogurt in the egg soak, this French toast is not as sweet as the standard recipe your grandmother made. The citrus works well with every seasonal berry you can imagine, as well as fresh banana slices or peaches, so this colorful breakfast can change with the seasons. This makes about two servings, but that depends on the size of the bread slices you use.

Sunday Fruited French Toast

DIRECTIONS:

In a pie pan or shallow baking dish, beat the eggs with a fork. Add the remaining ingredients and stir to combine.

Soak the bread slices in the batter for approximately 5 minutes, turning the bread once. The chia will cling to the toast from the egg wash.

In a large skillet with medium heat, melt the butter and cook the slices of bread until crispy brown.

Top with the fruit of your choice and, if you want, dust with confectioners' sugar for a pretty presentation.

This is great for kids and guests, too. Everyone can choose their favorite topping if several fruits are in season at once. This toast also works well seasoned with a sprinkle of cinnamon or with a touch of honey or maple syrup.

2 eggs

½ cup Greek yogurt

¼ cup milk (cow, goat, almond, or soy will work)

1 tablespoon orange juice concentrate

1 teaspoon orange zest

1 dash of nutmeg

2 tablespoon butter

1 teaspoon chia

1 baguette or ciabatta bread sliced to about ¾ inch thickness

seasonal fruit of your choice

Pre-packaged oatmeal (often sold as a packet) can have a surprising amount of sugar. The varieties marketed toward kids can even include things like gummy candy, marshmallows, high fructose corn syrup-based "fruit syrups," or sugar-based sprinkles. Several types of granola bars have the sugar equivalent of a regular candy bar. When you're looking over the instant oatmeal packets in the store, be sure to look where the sugar is listed on the ingredients panel. Usually it's in second place, right behind the oats!

If you're eating oatmeal for breakfast, you're trying to do something good for yourself or your family. You don't need HFCS or sugar sneaking around sabotaging your efforts. This makes one serving of oatmeal.

Almost Instant Chia Oatmeal

DIRECTIONS:

Add the filtered water to your oats in a microwave-safe cup. You don't even need to stir; simply microwave for about 50–60 seconds. Carefully remove from microwave and stir. Now you can add your choice of toppings. Granola adds great crunch, while any of the fruits add a touch of sweetness.

½ cup of quick cooking oats

1 cup filtered water (plus a splash more)

1 teaspoon of dry chia

Your choice of "sprinkles," such as nuts, dried fruit, fresh fruit, or granola

{ Need more fiber and a little crunch? Add 1 teaspoon dry chia as a "sprinkle" on top. Want sweeter oatmeal? Need to get kids to eat it? You can sweeten with agave nectar. It's lower on the glycemic index than sugar, and doesn't have the side effects of aspartame. Fresh fruit can really up the sweetness factor as well. }

{ There are many discussions about steel cut oats vs. rolled oats vs. quick cooking oats. You may lose some of the fiber in quick cooking oats, but 20 minutes to cook steel cut oatmeal is about 19 minutes too long for us. If something takes too long, or is inconvenient, it becomes a nuisance and is then generally dropped from the menu. You're making up for the fiber by adding chia, so it doesn't have to be a big worry for you. }

For those of us watching our cholesterol and unhealthy fats, deviled eggs are a bit scary. No more! These deviled eggs are yolkless and filled with satisfying flavor. The fillings are savory and easy to make with just a bowl and a fork. The avocado filling is smooth and brings beneficial vegetable folate and heart-healthy unsaturated fat. The sweet potato filling is a little spicy with paprika and a bit of mustard. Makes 12 deviled eggs.

To make the eggs…
Place 6 eggs in a medium saucepan and fill the water level to about one inch over the eggs. Bring to a boil, and then lower the heat to just a simmer for 5 minutes. Remove from heat and let stand for 10 minutes. When the eggs have cooled, you may gently crack and peel. Cut each peeled egg in half, and remove the yolk, leaving an empty hollow for the filling. Discard the yolks. While you are cooking the eggs, you can make these easy fillings.

No Yolk Deviled Eggs: Sweet Potato and Avocado

DIRECTIONS:

Avocado filling:

Smash up the avocado in a small bowl with a fork, then mince and smash the garlic clove to release the flavor and aroma. Add all the other ingredients to the bowl and stir to blend. To avoid a mess while filling the egg whites and scoop quickly, you can use a small ice cream or cookie scoop. Place 1 scoop of filling where the yolk used to be in each egg half. Chill until ready to serve.

Sweet Potato filling:

Use a fork to prick the sweet potato skin multiple times to let the steam out. Then place in the microwave for about 5 minutes to cook all the way through. Let cool slightly and remove the peel. Smash in a small bowl with a fork, and then add the remaining ingredients.

Stir to blend everything together. A large melon ball utensil or small ice cream scoop will make for easy filling. Chill until ready to serve. Sprinkle with a little paprika for the traditional look of these deliciously deviled eggs.

You can easily make these on the weekend and refrigerate for a "grab 'n' go" breakfast any day of the week.

Avocado filling:
1 ripe avocado peeled and seed removed
1 clove garlic smashed and minced
1 or 2 plum tomatoes chopped
1 tablespoon of dried basil
1 tablespoon dry chia
1 teaspoon white balsamic vinegar
Small dash of hot sauce if desired

Sweet Potato Filling:
1 small sweet potato
1 tablespoon Dijon mustard
½ cucumber, diced
1 teaspoon smoked paprika
Small dash of hot sauce if desired
1 tablespoon dry chia

Some muffins are strictly breakfast muffins, while others can make a tasty dessert! This muffin is satisfactory for either category. It's sweet and moist thanks to the use of a whole sweet potato in the recipe. It may sound a little unusual to add this healthy root to a muffin, but the results are super! The muffins don't end up tasting at all like the potato, and they are a kid favorite with their orange color. We admit it: we are chocoholics. These muffins are filled with fiber, flavor, and chocolate! They are extremely moist and just what you were hoping a muffin could be. Depending on the sweetness of your chosen potato, they may be a bit rich for breakfast, so a fun alternative can be cinnamon chips. This makes 12 medium size muffins.

Sunny Sweet Potato and Chocolate Chip Chia Muffins

DIRECTIONS:

Preheat the oven to 400 degrees and spray the muffin tin. We use paper liners as those darn chips may stick to the bottom of the cups even though they were sprayed with cooking spray.

Microwave the sweet potato for approximately 4 minutes. Let it rest to finish cooking and cooling while you put the rest of the ingredients together.

Combine the flour, sugar, baking powder, cinnamon, and salt in a large bowl. Stir to distribute the dry ingredients.

Open and scrape out the cooked sweet potato to equal ½ cup. In a small bowl, place the smashed sweet potato, milk, butter, egg, and chia gel. Stir to combine. Pour the wet ingredients over the dry and stir to combine just until moistened. Stir in chocolate chips.

Spoon the batter into the prepared muffin cups to about ¾ full.

Bake for 20 minute or until a wooden pick comes out clean. Cool for 5 minutes and then remove from pan and let them cool on a wire rack.

1 sweet potato (large enough to get ½ cup cooked potato about 5" long by 3" across)
1½ cups all purpose flour
2 teaspoons baking powder
⅓ cup brown sugar
1 teaspoon cinnamon
dash salt
¾ cup milk
4 tablespoons melted butter
1 egg
3 tablespoons chia gel
½ cup chocolate chips

Here's an interesting old-fashioned breakfast with a fun new twist. You have to make this in a cast-iron skillet (or pan with an oven-safe handle) and it's not quite a pancake and not really a popover. What is it exactly? It's delicious! The batter wrinkles up in the pan causing a light and thin (yet slightly crisp) "pancake" to form as it bakes. This makes one crumple, which you can divide into slices in your choice of sizes.

Breakfast Chia Crumple

DIRECTIONS:

First, preheat the oven to 425 degrees. Add all ingredients to one bowl and use a mixer to beat them together. Alternately, you can use a blender. If you're making the "citrus" version, add in the two teaspoons of zest and mix again.

Once the oven has heated, place 2 tablespoons of the butter into the skillet and put it in the oven to melt. As soon as the butter has melted down (about 2 minutes) remove the skillet and tilt it so the butter coats the entire bottom. Pour in the batter, and if you're adding mini chips and blueberries, now is the time to sprinkle them in. Now, return the skillet to the oven.

Bake this for 10 minutes at 425 degrees, then turn down the oven to 350 and bake for another 10–15 minutes. When done it will be wrinkly, crumply, and golden brown. It will crumple in a different way each time you make it.

3 tablespoons butter

1 tablespoon gelled chia seeds

⅔ cup skim milk

½ cup flour

1 tablespoon honey

2 eggs

¼ teaspoon salt

Optional Ingredients

1 teaspoon lemon zest

1 teaspoon orange zest

fresh blueberries

fresh strawberries

chocolate mini-chips (if you feel like making it as a dessert instead)

This versatile breakfast can be served with light syrup, berries, jam, or just about anything you like! However, by itself, the crumple cake is very mild. Try it with the zest and topping first.

You can also try our cottage cheese spread. To make the spread, just combine the following in a small bowl:
2 tablespoons frozen orange juice concentrate
½ cup low fat (or 1%) cottage cheese
1 tablespoon powdered sugar.

To serve, cut into slices as you would a pizza. If it doesn't all get eaten right away, you can wrap it up once it cools. The next day, it can be re-heated by cutting into slices and placing in the toaster or toaster oven. It will crisp up again, but the crumples may flatten out.

This simple healthy breakfast bar is amazingly easy to make, and you can eat it all week long without having the same thing twice. Simply prepare it on the weekend and top with any number of your favorite mix-n-match toppings. You can also add mix-ins to the bars themselves for even more variety. If you think breakfast is boring, this is a great one to try! This makes one 8 x 8 pan of oat squares, which you can divide into about 9 squares.

Easy Chia Oat Squares

DIRECTIONS:

This is so easy, you only need one bowl. Simply mix together all the ingredients listed above by stirring. Add any mix-in from the list you may want. Turn out into a greased 8 x 8 pan, and either cover and refrigerate to bake the next day or bake at 350 degrees for 25–30 minutes.

When done, the edges may turn light golden brown and cracks may appear on the surface.

If you try to remove it from the pan right away, it will crumble and can be served in a bowl. If you wait for it to cool, it can be cut into bars. The bars themselves (without mix-ins) are simple and very lightly sweet, but the amount of mix and match topping that you can do ensures you won't eat the same thing twice in a week!

This is a great way to get kids to eat their oatmeal without resorting to expensive and sugary store-bought packs.

Toppings shown here: Strawberries, apple and plain yogurt, blueberries and blueberry yogurt, and peanut butter and banana. A touch of honey or maple syrup works well, too. You can even scramble an egg and place it on top. The chia also adds in extra fiber, so you can still enjoy the protein from eggs without having to worry about your daily fiber.

Dry Ingredients
1½ cups quick cooking oats
½ cup brown sugar
1 teaspoon baking powder
pinch salt

Wet Ingredients
½ cup nonfat milk
1 egg
2 tablespoons melted butter
2 teaspoons vanilla
2 tablespoons gelled chia seeds

Optional Mix-ins
raisins (regular or golden)
dried cranberries
2 teaspoons cinnamon
dried berries or dried cherries
2 tablespoons maple syrup

Peanut butter is full of protein, so it's a good pick for breakfast! This is an easy waffle recipe that will work in a regular or Belgian waffle maker. How many waffles it makes depends on the size of your waffle iron. The "very peanut" flavor of these waffles comes from the use of all-natural unsweetened peanut butter. You may have to stir it, and you may have to keep it in the fridge, but this pure/natural peanut butter really piles on the flavor and will save you from consuming high fructose corn syrup or loads of sugar.

For topping these waffles, don't reach for the maple syrup (it's not as good). Anything that goes well with a P&J will be delicious here. Fruits like strawberries, raspberries, or banana slices work very well. A drizzle of honey is delightful and makes a great presentation. You can even spread on some of your favorite jam.

Peanut Butter Chia Waffles

DIRECTIONS:

First, separate the eggs. Place the yolks in a small bowl and the whites into a deep cup or bowl. Use a hand mixer to beat the egg whites to stiff peaks. Set the whites aside, and use the hand mixer to combine the egg yolks, butter, peanut butter, and brown sugar in a small bowl. The mixture will be brown and thick.

Next mix together the flour, baking powder, and salt. Add the milk to the peanut butter mixture and it will loosen. Mix with the mixer until well combined. Last, stir the chia gel into the peanut butter mixture by hand. Add the wet ingredients to the dry, and stir to combine. Fold in the egg whites, and you're ready to pour the batter into the waffle iron.

Waffles are done when lightly browned and crisp. These waffles are very filling. They're not an ultra-light little buffet style waffle, so you'll likely only want one or a half. If there are leftover waffles, you can put them in a bag and heat in the toaster on the following day. They crisp up again quite well!

1 ¼ cup flour
2 tablespoons brown sugar
½ teaspoons salt
½ teaspoons baking powder
2 tablespoons butter
2 tablespoons chia gel
¼ cup peanut butter
2 eggs
¾ cup milk

Fluffy citrus pancakes with special sauce! Looking for a new and healthier twist on pancakes? Or maybe a special breakfast? Try these light and lemony pancakes with anti-oxidant blueberry sauce instead of syrup and butter. Using fresh lemon juice and zest really makes a difference. Since zest is required, it's easy to just juice the lemons. To make heart-shaped pancakes, brush the inside of a cookie cutter with oil and place on griddle. Pour batter into cookie cutters and wait until batter begins to bubble. Remove cookie cutters before flipping. This recipe makes about 16 pancakes, depending on the size.

Lemon Chia Cheesecake Pancakes

DIRECTIONS:

Sift together flour, sugar, baking powder, baking soda, and salt in a bowl. In a medium size bowl, use a whisk to combine the whole egg, ricotta cheese, egg whites, dry chia, lemon juice, lemon zest, and 1 tablespoon of oil. Use a wooden spoon to fold together all ingredients to make the batter. Use cooking spray on a skillet and you're ready to cook.

When the skillet is ready, pour the batter in about ¼ cup measures. When the pancakes begin to bubble in the middle and dry at the edges (about 2 minutes), they're ready to flip. Pancakes should be light brown on both sides when finished.

To make the blueberry sauce, in a small saucepan, add the blueberries, sugar, water, and salt. While waiting for the mixture to boil, use a small bowl and mix together the lemon juice and cornstarch. As soon as it boils, reduce the heat and add the lemon juice mixture. Simmer about 2 minutes until it thickens slightly (will be bubbly).

1 cup flour

2 tablespoons sugar

2 teaspoons baking powder

½ teaspoon baking soda

¼ teaspoon salt

1 cup part skim ricotta cheese

1 egg

2 egg whites

½ cup fresh squeezed lemon juice

4 teaspoons fine lemon zest

1 tablespoon oil

1 tablespoon dry chia

Blueberry Sauce:

⅔ tablespoon fresh lemon juice

1 teaspoon corn starch

1 cup frozen (or fresh) blueberries

¼ cup sugar

1 tablespoon water

⅛ teaspoons salt

Smoothies can be made out of any of the fruits and veggies you have in the house. We always suggest using a banana to put a little natural sugar and creaminess in your lovely beverage. Start your morning off right with a jump on your "quota" of fruits and veggies. You could have half in the morning and save half for the afternoon if you fall into an energy slump. When using whole fruits you get lots of fiber and lots of satisfying taste. Experiment and find out what you like! A smoothie is a great way to stay feeling full longer. Need more "fullness-factor?" You can add just about as much chia as you want to each of these smoothies. Want to up the protein by 20 grams? You can add packaged whey to your smoothie. Remember: A blender is not a calorie-eliminator. Each smoothie will still have exactly the same amount of calories as the fruits that went into making it, so plan to make the smoothie your whole meal. The objective is to fill up on fruit and chia without accidentally overeating by adding other items to the breakfast menu.

3 Chia Smoothies for you!

Fresh And Delicious Watermelon and Lime Chia Smoothie

2 cups chunked watermelon
½ cup Greek yogurt
½ lime (zest and juice)
2 tablespoons chia gel

Zest the ½ lime and squeeze the juice into your blender or food processor. Add the chunked watermelon pieces, yogurt, lime, and chia gel. Blend. Done! These ingredients will make about 3 four-ounce smoothies.

Bright And Early Mango, OJ, and Strawberry Chia Smoothie

1 mango (fresh or frozen)
2 cups orange juice
1 banana
½ cup strawberries
2 tablespoons chia gel

Put all the ingredients in the blender or food processor. Blend. You may want to add a little ice to your smoothie. These ingredients make about 4 four-ounce smoothies.

Lean and Green Great Tasting Chia Smoothie

Handful of green grapes
2 handfuls of spinach (stems removed) or dark green leafy veggie of your choice
1 cup orange juice
1 banana
2 tablespoons of chia gel

Put all the ingredients in the blender or food processor. Blend. These ingredients make about 4 four-ounce smoothies.

Keep the blender or food processor on the kitchen counter because making smoothies is so convenient and easy.

These easy sausages taste great at breakfast, lunch, or dinner. Use them with an egg for breakfast, place on a bun for lunch, or serve on a roll or in a pita pocket with a slice of tomato for dinner. This makes about eight small patties.

Protein in the morning gives you energy for your day, but traditional pork sausage can contain lots of salt, saturated fat, or over-processed meat. These are made with ground turkey and healthy seasonings.

Spicy Chia Sausage Patties

DIRECTIONS:

In a medium bowl, add the half cup of canned, rinsed, and drained black beans. Smash the beans with a fork. Add the 1 pound of ground turkey. Dice the apple into small pieces, and snip the parsley. Grate the fresh ginger and add all of the remaining seasonings. Last, add the chia and mix by hand to combine. Pull apart, and shape the mixture into six patties.

To cook, use a large skillet and medium heat. Heat skillet and add 1 tablespoon olive oil. When the oil is hot, place the patties carefully into the skillet. Cook on the first side for about 4 minutes, flip, and cook for another 4 minutes.

This makes the exterior brown and crispy, without using lots of oil. Once you taste these, you'll want to try lots of different ways to serve them. These sausages taste great with an egg or even spicy mustard. You can enjoy plain or with your choice of buns.

Dry Ingredients

1 pound ground turkey
1 small green apple
1 tablespoon dry chia
½ cup canned black beans
1 handful parsley

Seasonings

½ teaspoon ground sage

½ teaspoon ground thyme

¾ teaspoons red pepper flakes

1 tablespoon fresh ginger (grated)

1 pinch salt (optional)

For Cooking

1 tablespoon olive oil

Let breakfast be a boost for your health! If you get 5 grams of protein and 5 grams of fiber, your energy and digestion will be much better for the day.

With the market flooded by sugary cereals, bland white bread, and deep-fried donuts, it's time to make a healthy change. This low fat patty has added protein and fiber from the chia, and when you choose a multi grain bun, you'll boost the fiber as well.

These waffles are lightly textured and easy to make. They're very versatile, too. You can top a plain waffle with almost anything. Here, you can use great fresh fruit selections, as well as a cinnamon or orange chia topping. How many waffles it makes depends on the size of your waffle iron or if it is a Belgian waffle maker.

Quick and Versatile Chia Waffles

DIRECTIONS:

First, separate the eggs and beat the egg whites until stiff peaks form. Set the whites aside, and in another bowl combine all of the dry ingredients by stirring. Once your waffle iron has heated up and is ready to use, begin adding the wet ingredients to the dry. Use your hand mixer to combine well. Last, fold in the egg whites, and you're ready to ladle the batter into your waffle iron. Waffles are done when lightly browned and crisp in texture.

Serve with chocolate chia orange sauce (page 177) or with Chia Cinnamon Sauce (recipe below).

Chia Cinnamon Sauce:

1 green tart apple, diced
½ cup brown sugar
1 teaspoon cinnamon
2 tablespoons water
1 tablespoon butter
1 teaspoon chia

In a glass measuring cup, place the sugar, cinnamon, butter, water, and chia. Microwave for 40 seconds. Stir the mixture. Microwave again to melt the sugar. Cool for a few minutes and add the diced apple. Stir to coat the apple pieces. Now you're ready to use this cinnamon-ey syrup on waffles, pancakes, or French toast. The crisp, tart apple is a great contrast with the sweet cinnamon.

Dry Ingredients

2 cups flour
1 tablespoon baking powder
½ teaspoons salt
1 tablespoon sugar

Wet Ingredients

2 egg whites
2 egg yolks
2 cups milk (goat, cow, or rice will work)
3 tablespoons oil
3 tablespoons chia gel

Beware! Thanks to the high fiber content, these muffins are very filling and may even delay your lunch if you decide to have one for breakfast. The chia has soluble and insoluble fiber, and the bran flakes add even more fiber. Fiber isn't digested by the body and it doesn't add to your calorie count. All it does is take up space in the digestive system and help keep food moving smoothly. Both of these factors help you feel full.

Traditional muffins and fast food muffins often derive their texture from lots of sugar and butter. These muffins rely on the sweetness and moistness of tasty fruit to bring the expected texture to the table. If you're looking for an easy bite in the morning that will give you a great start to your fiber goal for the day, mix up a batch of these muffins.

Banana Bran Chia Muffins

Makes about 1 dozen medium muffins.

DIRECTIONS:

Preheat oven to 375 degrees and coat your muffin tin with cooking spray.

In a small bowl, stir together the dry ingredients. In another bowl cream the butter and brown sugar together until light and grainy. Add the eggs and beat to incorporate. Next add the milk, chia gel, and apple sauce. Blend in the smashed bananas. Stir in the dry ingredients.

Bake for 20–25 minutes. Let the muffins stand in the tin for 5 minutes. Place muffins on a rack to finish cooling.

1½ cup all purpose flour
½ cup crushed plain bran flakes
1 teaspoon baking powder
1 teaspoon baking soda
dash salt
4 tablespoons of butter
¼ cup apple sauce
¼ cup brown sugar
4 tablespoons chia gel
¼ cup milk
2 eggs
2–3 smashed ripe bananas depending upon their size

{ Not that we think that there will be very many muffins left after a day or two, but do remember that there are no preservatives. (Didn't see any in the list, did you?) So you may want to freeze a few and warm one up in the microwave on a day when you deserve a treat. }

Chia Side Dishes, Sandwiches, and Burgers

A chia side dish is a great way to add nutrition to any meal. These super sides can be matched up with meat, paired with a different chia side, or used as a compliment for something else you already like to eat. Some sides can sabotage a meal, adding an unhealthy burden to the plate or piling on calories that don't do you much good. Smart, easy, and delicious alternatives are at your fingertips with these tasty sides and sandwiches.

Looking for lunch? Some of these sides, if there are leftovers, can easily be taken for a convenient lunch the following day. The sandwiches, wraps, and burgers can also be great for lunch, at home or at work.

With these sides, what you see is what you get. There are no ingredient panels on a tomato. There are no additives or preservatives in strawberries. Every ingredient is a word you can say, not some unpronounceable chemical. You won't want to go back to powdered cheese, canned meat, or over-cooked, over-processed anything after trying these sides.

Chia-enhanced sides will compliment any meal. Just choose one or two side dishes and up your fullness factor and fruit/vegetable quota for the day! Enjoying a large variety of tastes and textures will add so much joy to your meals.

Almost nothing could be more fresh and simple. Taking advantage of seasonal fruits and vegetables is the key to retaining the nutrients in your foods and saving grocery dollars. Enjoying a large variety of foods almost guarantees that you will obtain all the nutrients your body needs to stay healthy. There's no heavy mayo in this coleslaw. It has fresh yogurt, with a kick from the nutmeg. Healthy, crunchy cabbage provides maximum benefits, while the pear and tangerine are an unusual, but colorful and fitting addition to this recipe.

Easy Creamy Pear Coleslaw

Makes about 4 side dish-size portions.

2 cups shredded coleslaw mix with carrot

½ cup Greek style yogurt

1 tangerine or orange sections

1 pear

dash of nutmeg

1 small handful fresh parsley

1 teaspoon dry chia

DIRECTIONS:

In a bowl combine the coleslaw mix, yogurt, and cubed pear. Zest the orange or tangerine. Cut open your citrus fruit of choice, and remove the sections to place in the bowl. Stir in the chia, nutmeg, and fresh parsley. Simply stir to combine, and you're ready to serve. This is fantastic chilled for lunch or as a side.

If pears are out of season you could use canned pears in natural juice if need be.

This festive salad needs to marinate for about 20 minutes so you will want to plan ahead, but it is worth it! If you don't have raspberry vinegar in the house, see the note at the bottom of page 53 to make your own. Besides tasting great in this dressing, mushrooms are high in micro-nutrients and fiber. Explore your grocery store and shake up your menus! Strawberry and mushroom may seem like an odd combination, but the great seasoned marinade really brings the flavors together. A great variety of textures and tastes make this a fun and unique salad. This makes two medium dinner salads.

Portobello Mushroom and Chia Strawberry Salad

DIRECTIONS:

In a pie plate or baking dish, combine the olive oil, garlic, basil, honey, vinegar, mustard, and chia. With a spoon, stir to combine all. Place the mushroom sections in the marinade. Coat and let stand for 20 minutes so they soak in the flavors.

In a bowl place the strawberries, celery, onion, and mixed greens. Pour the mushrooms and all the marinade on top and stir to combine. It's as simple as that! You're ready to serve.

You can sometimes find raspberry vinegar in the specialty vinegar area of your supermarket. Not all markets may have it, and when you find it, it may be a little pricey. Want to make your own at home? It's so easy with this mini recipe:

*To make raspberry vinegar: Pour ½ cup of white vinegar into a small bowl and add ¼ cup raspberries (fresh or frozen). Allow vinegar and berries to steep over night. The following day, use a spoon to smash up the berries in the vinegar, to maximize the juice and flavor. Using a sieve, strain the raspberry pulp and pour the vinegar into a clean, lidded glass jar. It's important to not use plastic around strong substances like vinegar, as it can pull chemicals out of the plastic and into your food. You will be surprised how often you reach for your fruited vinegar when making fresh salads.

¼ cup olive oil

1 garlic clove smashed and diced finely

1 teaspoon dried basil

2 teaspoons of honey

2 teaspoons of raspberry–flavored vinegar*

2 teaspoon Dijon mustard

1 teaspoons dry chia

1 Portobello mushroom quartered and sliced into

½ inch sections

3 rings red onion sliced into sections

1 celery stalk diced

small handful of sliced strawberries

greens of choice

Wouldn't it be fun to surprise your family with a "pink" side dish! The chopped cranberries turn this couscous pink! We serve this side with our favorite grilled chicken and a fresh green salad. It's easy and a little crunchy and packed with flavor as well as festive color. With cranberries, apple, and spicy ginger this is a tasty side with a bit of tart flavor to enjoy. This makes four side dishes.

Cranberry Chia Couscous

DIRECTIONS:

Prepare the couscous according to package directions. In a small food processor, pulse the cranberries to chop into small pieces, but don't pulverize. Cut the orange in half and remove the orange sections. Reserve any juice in a bowl. Rinse and drain the chickpeas. Combine the chopped green apple, chickpeas, orange sections, red onion, and parsley in a bowl.
In a measuring cup, add the oil, cranberries, the reserved orange juice (from the sectioned orange, should be about 2 tablespoons), grated ginger, chia, nuts or seeds, and honey. Stir to combine. "Fluff" the couscous and add to the bowl. Stir to combine. Pour your "dressing" over the contents of the bowl. Gently stir to coat the ingredients, being careful not to over mix. Now you can "think pink" for a fresh take on couscous!

½ cup couscous

¼ cup fresh or frozen (if frozen, slightly defrosted) chopped cranberries

½ small green apple

½ can chickpeas (freeze the other ½ for another use)

1 orange

1 tablespoons olive oil

1 teaspoon honey

1 tablespoon chopped red onion

small handful of parsley, stems removed and chopped

1 teaspoon dry chia

1 teaspoon fresh ginger, grated

nuts or seeds of choice

This is a sweet and spicy refreshing salad. With fresh plums, crunchy celery, and cool cucumber, it's very easy to make but has a festive colorful presentation on the plate. You can use it as a side when you serve over spinach or garden greens. Makes four servings.

Plum Chia Salad

DIRECTIONS:

First, cut the plums into bite-size pieces. Then dice the celery and the cucumber. Make sure to vary the size of the pieces for a fun, festive look. Place all the pieces in a medium bowl and add the spinach or garden greens.

Mince the garlic and add it to a measuring cup along with the lime juice, honey, grated fresh ginger, and chia seeds. Stir to combine. Pour the mixture over the vegetables in the bowl and mix well to distribute the flavors.

Dry Ingredients
3 plums

1 small cucumber

1 or 2 stalks of celery

2 cups baby spinach or greens

2 teaspoons dry chia seeds

Seasonings
2 tablespoons lime juice

1 tablespoon honey

2 teaspoons minced garlic

1 teaspoon fresh grated ginger

Lively! Crunchy! Here's a cool, crisp side salad to add color to any meal. The flavors of ginger, lemon, and apple are a great compliment. It's made with shredded fresh cabbage, so you get the nutritional benefits of this great veggie. Chia and black beans add plant protein with antioxidants. This makes about six sides.

Ginger Crisp Chia Salad

DIRECTIONS:

First, rinse and drain the canned black beans. In a large bowl, add the 3 cups coleslaw mix, then dice the red pepper and add it to the bowl. Grate the fresh ginger (about 1 inch of ginger root) and snip the parsley tops and add to the bowl. Last, cut up the apple (as it will turn brown) into bite-size pieces. Stir all dry ingredients together in the bowl.

After zesting, juice the lemon into a cup. If there is not enough juice for ¼ cup, top it off with apple cider vinegar. Add the honey and stir in the zest and chia seeds. Pour over the salad mixture in the bowl and mix to dress the salad.

Dry Ingredients
3 cups shredded coleslaw mix
1 small green apple
1 small red sweet pepper
½ cup black beans
1 teaspoon grated ginger
1 handful parsley zest from
1 lemon
1 tablespoon dry chia seeds

Wet Ingredients
1 teaspoon honey
juice of 1 lemon

Ginger is known for its immune system boosting properties, but did you know about the cancer-fighting potential of raw cabbage? Sinigrin is one of the cabbage glucosinolates that keeps appearing in great anti-cancer studies, especially for breast, bladder, and colon cancer help. The key to getting all the benefits from cabbage, though, is leaving it raw.

If you can microwave a frozen brick of chopped broccoli or spinach you can quickly prepare this mock soufflé. Once the frozen veggie of choice has been warmed/thawed and drained, just dump the other ingredients into the casserole, stir, and in about 10 minutes this cheesy side dish is ready. This can be used as a dinner dip or a faux-soufflé side. This is a good dip or side for two people.

Faux Spinach Soufflé

DIRECTIONS:

In a covered casserole dish, microwave the brick of chopped spinach or broccoli for 3–4 minutes to thaw. Drain by pressing out the water with a fork. Remove half of the veggie and refreeze or save for another recipe. Place the remaining ingredients into the casserole and stir to combine. Microwave for approximately 10 minutes on 50 percent power or until almost set in the center. Let stand for a few minutes to finish setting.

If desired, you can top with a shake of parmesan cheese.

This "soufflé" for two can be doubled easily to serve four. If you decide to double, then you will have a start on lunch tomorrow! Just bring a few crackers and some vegetable sticks and you're ready to crunch with lunch.

½ package (10 oz) frozen chopped broccoli or spinach

1 tablespoon all-purpose flour

1 egg

¾ cup shredded white cheddar cheese

½ cup low fat small curd cottage cheese

1 tablespoon dry chia

dash pepper

Looking for a summery, colorful side dish? Look no further than this super apple chia salad. It's wholesome, filling, and looks pretty in a bowl or on a plate. Plus, with the creamy "dressing" and two kinds of apples, even picky-eaters will enjoy this new twist on the side-salad. This makes about four small sides.

Awesome Apple Chia Salad

DIRECTIONS:

First, prepare the apples by chopping them into bite-sized pieces. Using 2 different kinds of apples for this recipe (tart and sweet) really gives it a unique twist. Place the apple pieces, broccoli slaw, and carrot slices in a large bowl, and get a small bowl to make the dressing.

In the small bowl, combine the non-fat sour cream, apple juice concentrate, dry chia, sugar, and lemon juice. Stir or whisk to thoroughly mix, then pour this over the mixture in the large bowl. Stir to coat all the pieces thoroughly. Stir again and the seeds will cling to the dressing and begin to gel.

You're ready to serve! The dressing isn't runny, so this can be served on a plate or in a bowl. With its confetti-like look and colors, it's a great way to add a splash of fun to any meal. You can serve this plain or over your favorite greens. Since the dressing uses fat free sour cream, there's no fat to be found, and it will still help fill you up.

½ cup granny smith apples, coarsely chopped

½ cup coarsely chopped gala apples

2 tablespoons non-fat sour cream

1 teaspoon dry chia seeds

1 tablespoon frozen apple juice concentrate (thawed)

1 teaspoon lemon juice

1 teaspoon sugar OR half teaspoon stevia

½ cup sliced carrot

⅔ cup shredded broccoli-slaw OR

⅓ cup each shredded red and green cabbage

{ Broccoli slaw comes in a bag in most supermarket's produce sections. It's pre-made and pre-shredded for convenience. It will usually have strips of broccoli, carrot, and sometimes red cabbage. When something is as easy as chop, pour, and stir, healthy meals are a breeze! }

You may have heard of tabbouleh, or even bought a little pricey package in the store, but did you know it's as good for you as it is tasty? Now you can make this fresh-tasting dish any time you want. This recipe makes about four servings, but can easily be doubled if you need more.

Chia Tabbouleh Salad

DIRECTIONS:

First, prepare the bulgur wheat. Simply pour the bulgur into a heat-safe dish and, using the microwave, heat ¾ cup of water to a boil, then pour it over the bulgur. Cover the dish and let it stand for 30 minutes. Because the stove isn't involved, you can go do something else while you wait!

This process will soften the bulgur. While it is soaking, you may want to prepare the rest of the ingredients.

As long as you can chop and toss, you can make this simple salad! Dice the tomato half, the cucumber, and the onion. Then, chop the fresh parsley and mint. You can use dried mint if fresh is not available, but fresh parsley must be used. Fresh mint maximizes the great taste!

½ cup bulgur wheat
½ tomato
¼ cup peeled cucumber
¼ cup red onion
¼ cup fresh parsley
¼ cup fresh mint

Dressing Ingredients

⅛ cup extra virgin olive oil
1 tablespoon fresh lemon juice
¼ teaspoon kosher salt
⅛ teaspoons black pepper
1 teaspoon dry chia seeds

In a small bowl, combine the dressing ingredients and stir to mix well. Scoop the chopped vegetables on top of the parsley and mint mixture, top with the dressing and bulgur, and toss gently until thoroughly coated.

Tabbouleh can be eaten as a side salad or used as a dip. In the Middle East where it originated, it was eaten by scooping it onto a lettuce leaf, but pita pieces, chips, and vegetable slices can also be used.

{ Did you know…? Combining foods can sometimes increase their healthy effects. This is called "food synergy." Healthy oils, such as olive or avocado, help the body absorb phytochemicals. These chemicals have a protective effect for your health. The healthy oil makes nutrients in the food more available for the body to use. In this case, the olive oil helps release the lycopene in the tomatoes. }

Served over a bed of fresh spinach and loaded with healthy vegetables, this isn't your usual pasta salad. Jalapeño peppers heat it up while the orzo pasta helps blend all the flavors together for a memorable side dish that's great for you, too! (As a side, this makes about six servings; for larger servings it will make about four.)

Spicy Orzo and Veggie Chia Salad

DIRECTIONS:

First, cook the pasta. Boil 6 cups of water in a large saucepan, then add the orzo. Cook for 10 to 12 minutes until tender. When done, rinse and drain.

While the pasta is cooking, you can mix the spices. Combine the oil, jalapeño, and chili powder in a medium bowl. Careful when mincing the pepper; they can irritate the skin and eyes, but though the capsaicin is good for digestion.

Next prepare the vegetables. Slice the carrot rounds thinly and break up the cauliflower and broccoli into smaller than bite-size pieces. Rinse and drain the black beans next, and if necessary, wash the spinach leaves as well.

Add the lemon and lime juice to the olive oil and spice mixture in the bowl, then pour in the orzo, chopped vegetables, and black beans. Stir all together to ensure everything is evenly seasoned. Sprinkle on the 1 tablespoon of dry chia while stirring. The seeds will cling to the various ingredients as you stir.

Divide the spinach leaves among your serving dishes. (As a side, this makes about six servings; for larger servings it will make about four.) Top the leaves with the orzo, vegetable, and bean mixture. The dish will be colorful, healthy, and filling, too!

¾ cup uncooked orzo pasta
⅓ cup thin-sliced carrot rounds
⅓ cup small broccoli pieces
⅓ cup small cauliflower pieces
½ can (8 oz) black beans (drained)
4 cups fresh spinach leaves
2 thin slices of red onion
2 tablespoons extra virgin olive oil
1 tablespoon minced jalapeño pepper
1 teaspoon chili powder
¼ cup fresh lime juice
¼ cup fresh lemon juice
1 tablespoon dry chia

You control the chia! How full do you want to be with this meal or side dish? You can use 1 dry tablespoon for the usual amount, 1½ tablespoon for maximum, or 1 teaspoon for a dish that's less filling, but still healthy.

Spicy! Cool! Summery! The tastes of summer freshen up every bite of this delicious salsa. You can serve this by itself as a side dish or with treats from the grill. This salsa tastes light and fresh with two summer melons, cucumber, and zesty lime. The dash of pepper provides the familiar heat while fresh mint gives it a unique, cool snap. Pair this up with one of our great chia burgers and feel full all evening long. This makes about four small sides.

Fun Melon Chia Salsa

DIRECTIONS:

It's important to use fresh mint* for this recipe. The flavor of this fresh herb blends so nicely with the other flavors that no one will want to miss out. Finely chop the mint and add it to the bowl. For a little heat, add a dash of cayenne pepper.

First, cut the melons and cucumbers into bite-sized cubes. If papaya is not in season, you can use a cantaloupe. Chop the cucumber and dice the onion. Place all the pieces into a large bowl.

Zest the limes and sprinkle the zest over the ingredients in the bowl, then squeeze all the juice into the bowl, too.

Sprinkle the chia and olive oil over the mixture and stir gently to thoroughly coat all ingredients. The chia seeds will cling among the mixture, helping blend the flavors and helping you to feel full. This is best served chilled.

Dry Ingredients

1 cup watermelon cubes

1 cup papaya (or cantaloupe) cubes

1 dash cayenne pepper

½ cup diced red onion

⅔ cup cucumber pieces

zest from 2 limes

3 tablespoons fresh mint leaves (finely chopped)*

1 tablespoon dry chia seeds

Wet Ingredients

2 tablespoons virgin olive oil

juice from

2 limes (or about 2 tablespoons)

Do you like things super hot? You can make this salsa a real blast with a teaspoon of fresh, minced jalapeño pepper. But beware if you keep this salsa overnight. The jalapeño will intensify over time and make this salsa much hotter. It may cover up the other flavors.

Colorful and healthy! Watermelons may be over 90 percent water, but they still have plenty of vitamin C and Lycopene—two great nutrients for your health. The redder, the better is the rule of thumb for watermelon selection and nutrition. Papaya has bromelian, an enzyme that helps you digest food more easily. If you use a cantaloupe, you'll get a healthy amount of vitamin C and A. Red onion contains both anthocyanins and quercetin, important anti-aging nutrients. Colorful food right from nature is not only beautiful, but also healthy.

This fantastic fruit salad is so refreshing and light! The fun bow ties and colorful fruit make it a pretty and delicious dish. The dressing has a special zing thanks to the orange zest that will really bring out the flavors of the ingredients. This makes six servings.

Bow Tie Pasta Salad

DIRECTIONS:

First, prepare the bow tie pasta by cooking according to the package directions. While the pasta is cooking, prepare the other ingredients. Cut the papaya or cantaloupe melon into half-inch cubes. Select your favorite cheese, and cut into ¼ inch cubes. The parsley can simply be chopped.

For the dressing, use a small bowl and add the mayonnaise, sour cream, honey, and gelled chia seeds with the orange zest. Stir to combine and your dressing is ready to use.

Rinse the pasta with cold water, drain, and put it in a large bowl. Add the rest of the ingredients to the bowl and pour the dressing over everything. Stir gently to mix and coat thoroughly. This can be served in a bowl or as a side on a plate. When you're ready to serve, you may want to sprinkle part of the 1 teaspoon of dry chia over the salad for a pretty look. (The gelled seeds tend to disappear into the dressing.) This is perfect for a hot summer day!

6 oz bow tie pasta
1 cup cantaloupe OR papaya
7 sprigs fresh parsley (chopped)
½ cup cubed mozzarella OR mild white cheddar

Dressing Ingredients

½ cup light mayonnaise
½ cup light sour cream
1 tablespoon honey
1 tablespoon gelled chia seeds
1 teaspoon dry chia seeds
1 teaspoon fresh orange zest

Need a salsa to compliment your meal of grilled chicken or fish? Or would you like to have a refreshing side salad that tickles your taste buds? Try this colorful and healthy recipe! Two kinds of peppers and chili powder spice it up while the cucumber and cilantro cool it down. The lime juice and zest help it taste fresh no matter how you use it. The MySeeds Chia test kitchen cooks are not "heat seekers," so depending on your heat tolerance, cut the amount of jalapeño pepper your family would like. This makes four small sides.

Zesty Lime Chia Salsa

DIRECTIONS:

If you need to cook an ear of corn, quickly and without boiling water, this is a great way to do it. Shuck it and de-string. Wrap the ear in wax paper and microwave it for about 2 minutes on high. Carefully remove your packaged corn. Unwrap the wax paper, avoiding any steam that may escape, and set aside to cool.

Next, in a large bowl, combine the beans and chopped vegetables. In a measuring cup, combine the olive oil, chili powder, lime juice, lime zest, and chia gel. Stir to combine, then pour over the other ingredients in the bowl. Now that the corn is cool enough to handle, remove the kernels with a knife and add to the bowl. Stir to coat the salsa. This can be served at room temperature or chilled if you prefer.

We serve this in a small bowl because the salsa has a higher liquid content. It can run into other foods on your plate if you don't use a bowl.

½ can of black beans (rinse and drained)

½ cucumber, seeded and chopped

1 ear of corn OR

¾ cup of canned/frozen corn

½ or less of 1 jalapeño pepper (depending on size) minced

¼ of 1 red pepper, diced

1 tablespoon chia gel

½ large tomato

Dressing

2 tablespoons olive oil

½ teaspoon chili powder

2 tablespoons chopped fresh cilantro

1 clove garlic, smashed and minced

1 teaspoon lime zest

Are you a burger lover? Are you a pizza lover, too? We have combined both for a sensational burger that we feel is top-notch. Whether you are using ground sirloin or ground turkey, this burger is loaded with all your favorite pizza spices. We have paired it with a flatbread to be reminiscent of the pizza dough crust and flattened the burger so it is easy to eat. A little shaved mozzarella on top will urge you to say "Mama Mia, that's a great burger!" This makes four standard size burgers.

The Pizza Burger

DIRECTIONS:

Place all burger ingredients in a medium bowl. Mix by hand to incorporate all the spices, chia, cheese, and tomato paste. Form into 4 evenly sized balls and then squash them flat to become about a 5-inch disc. Now you're ready to grill!

These burgers can be grilled inside or outside. To have that fun pizza-like appearance, and be a little different, we used a soft flatbread. This great pizza burger does not need a lot of bread wrapped around it. When the sirloin burgers have been cooked as you prefer them, move them to a plate. Briefly toast the flatbreads either on the grill or in the toaster. Now, spread a little tomato paste on the top slice of bread and sprinkle a little extra grated cheese on the burger. The hot burger will begin to melt the cheese. If you are using ground turkey, be sure to cook thoroughly, of course.

With the chia added to the burger mix, you will feel as if you just had a large Italian meal but you certainly didn't get the abundance of calories and carbohydrates. With one of your favorite fresh chia side dishes to compliment the burger, there will be no dessert for you . . . you'll be much too full. Hurray!

1 lb. ground sirloin or ground turkey

½ cup mozzarella cheese (grated as large pieces)

2 tablespoons tomato paste

1 teaspoon oregano

¼ teaspoon basil

2 teaspoons dry chia

⅛ teaspoon red pepper flakes

1 clove garlic minced (or ½ teaspoon garlic powder)

Additional tomato paste for topping

Additional grated mozzarella for topping

4 soft flatbreads, toasted or grilled briefly

You won't want to weigh your burger down with unhealthy toppings like bacon and mayonnaise when you see how unique and delicious this Chia Apple Turkey Burger is! With sweet-tart apple pieces, savory spices, and a crispy slice of apple to top it all off, this is one burger you'll want to keep on the menu! The ingredients listed make two turkey burgers.

Crispy Apple Chia Burger

DIRECTIONS:

⅔ lb lean ground turkey

juice from ½ of 1 lime

1 tablespoon apple cider vinegar

1 tablespoon brown sugar

½ tablespoons chopped mint leaves

1 teaspoon dry chia seeds

2 tablespoons basil dash of pepper

½ granny smith (tart) apple

1 scallion (white or light green part)

First, wash the apple thoroughly; it won't need to be peeled. Cut the apple into thin slices (as shown) but reserve two big, flat slices to go on top of the burger once it's finished. Kept raw, these slices will add a fantastic crunch and top off the fun flavor!

Chop the rest of the slices into tiny pieces; they will be mixed into and cooked with the turkey burgers.

Next, chop tiny pieces of the scallion, using only the white and light green parts. Place the ground turkey in a bowl and simply dump in the apple pieces, chopped scallion, spices, and vinegar. By hand, knead the mixture until everything is evenly distributed throughout the ground turkey.

Next, divide the mixture in half and form two burger patties. These can be grilled outdoors or on an indoor or stove-top grill. Grill thoroughly to ensure meat safety. Now, it can be topped with the large round apple slice from earlier.

You're ready to serve these unusual and delicious burgers! The unique mix of ingredients ensures these will be juicy, never dry. With chia seeds inside, the flavor will be enhanced, and you'll stay feeling full longer after you eat. By adding fiber with chia, you won't need to eat a high fiber roll unless you want to!

{ Did you know…? You may have read about "staying away from white breads" due to their high starchy content raising your blood sugar. The chia seed combats this effect when you eat it with meals. Chia slows down your body's conversion of carbohydrates into sugars, helping level out your blood sugar. When your blood sugar is kept even, you'll find you have more consistent energy throughout the day. }

A tasty burger without the meat! These hearty patties are totally meat free, so they're suitable for vegetarians. The colorful ingredients and tasty spices make these great with or without a bun. Add a roasted red pepper slice for fantastic flavor! This creates four large burgers.

Chia Garden Burgers

DIRECTIONS:

First, rinse and drain the chick peas, then add them to food processor. Mince the garlic clove. Then add all the spices to the food processor. Pulse until smooth.

Empty the bean mixture into a medium sized bowl. Put the carrot into the food processor and shred. By hand, cut the fresh spinach into smaller pieces and add to the bowl along with the shredded carrot.

With a large spoon, stir in the eggs and breadcrumbs until well combined.

By hand, divide into 4 to 6 patties. (Slider sized makes 6, regular burger size makes 4.) Flatten the patties to about ½ to ¾ inch so they will crisp on the outside when you cook them.

In a skillet on the stove top, preheat the 2 tablespoons olive oil. When the oil is hot, carefully lay the patties into the skillet. Cook for about 3 to 4 minutes on each side. When done, the outside should be lightly browned and slightly crisp.

Toppings: These are a real treat with roasted red pepper slices on top. You can also use avocado slices, fresh tomato, or even guacamole. They're spicy enough to eat plain, but toppings really send these "over the top."

Dry Ingredients

1 can chick peas/garbanzo beans (15 oz)
½ cup shredded carrot
¾ cup panko bread crumbs
1 clove garlic
1 tablespoon dry chia seeds
1½ cup fresh spinach
1 teaspoon smoked paprika
½ teaspoon coriander
½ teaspoon cumin
½ teaspoon red pepper flakes

Wet Ingredients

2 eggs
2 tablespoons olive oil

These burgers are a southwest sensation! Adding black beans to the ground turkey tastes great, adds more fiber, and means you use less meat. The burgers are seasoned with chili powder, and when you add the easy, zesty guacamole and a tomato slice, you've got a healthy hit! This recipe makes two regular size burgers.

Southwest Chia Bean Burgers

DIRECTIONS:

To prepare the burgers, place the rinsed and drained canned black beans in a large bowl and mash the beans. The mixture should be somewhat chunky. Add the egg, spices, chia seeds, and salt, then stir well to combine. Next, add the ground turkey and mix gently by hand until thoroughly combined. Over-mixing will result in tough burgers. Before cooking, the burger mixture will be very soft. Burger patties will become firmer as they cook. Divide the burger mixture into two equal parts and place on your prepared grilling surface. (A grill with a lid is ideal, since you won't have to flip the burgers.) Cook for about 4 minutes. When done, burger patties will be firm, lightly browned, and cooked all the way through.

While the burgers cook, you can make the extra-easy guacamole topping. It's so simple, but it tastes so fresh. First, mash up the avocado half with a fork until it's fairly smooth. Stir in the onion, lime juice, and the tablespoon of your favorite salsa, along with the salt. Mix well to combine, then refrigerate in a covered container until ready to use. The salsa you choose determines the heat. To serve, you can toast the buns in the toaster or in the broiler if you used it for the burgers. It's best to place the tomato slice on the bottom bun, and then add the burger patty. (This way it won't slide off. We learned the hard way.) Top the burger patty with a spoonful of guacamole topping, then add the top bun and you're ready to eat!

Burger Ingredients

½ pound lean ground turkey

2 burger buns

½ cup black beans (rinsed and drained)

1 tablespoon dry chia seeds

¼ teaspoon ground cumin

¼ teaspoon salt

1 tablespoon chili powder

1 egg

Topping Ingredients

1 tablespoon chopped sweet red onion

1 tablespoon of your favorite salsa

½ tablespoons lime juice

½ medium avocado

¼ teaspoon salt

2 tomato slices

Tip: These burgers are NOT recommended for the outdoor grill, since the burgers tend to crumble until cooked. If you do use an outdoor grill, line the grill with tin foil. If sprayed first with cooking oil spray, indoor mini-grills, skillet-style grills, and broiler pans all work well. The burgers flatten while cooking, and if the surface isn't clean, they can sometimes pull apart. If grilling multiple burgers, clean the grill between uses.

This easy pita can be prepared in no time and the portobello has an earthy/meaty taste to it. Most people have no idea how healthy mushrooms are for you! We just ate them because we like them. Did you know that mushrooms are low in calories and high in fiber, potassium, riboflavin, niacin, and selenium? It is all those micro-nutrients that add up to a healthy body.

Portobello Pepper Pita

DIRECTIONS:

Sautee veggies in a small skillet in the oil until tender/crisp. Once the vegetables are done, add to a bowl with your mixed greens of choice. Add a little "French Dressing" (see page 145) over the sautéed vegetables and greens, then toss to combine and coat in the tasty dressing. Warm the pita pocket in the microwave for a few seconds to prevent cracking or splitting. Cut it in half and carefully open it. Add a scoop of the salad mixture and you're ready to serve.

1 portobello cap sliced thickly

2 small sweet peppers sliced

1 small clove garlic smashed and diced

few rings of an onion sliced greens of choice

1 tablespoon of olive oil

1 whole pita pocket (cut in half)

This lighter, vegetarian wrap with zesty cannellini bean paste is perfect for lunch. Use your favorite flavor of tortilla, such as tomato, spinach, or traditional corn. You can even use a whole grain flat-bread (shown here).

These wraps are super easy to make. Just make the bean paste, add crunchy veggies of your choice, and you're ready to wrap. This makes about six average size tortillas.

Vegetarian Chia Lunch Wraps

DIRECTIONS:

First, rinse and drain the cannellini beans, then mince the garlic. In a food processor or blender, combine the beans, garlic, spices, cream cheese, and lemon juice. Pulse until smooth. If the mixture seems too dry, add ½ teaspoon filtered water. Add the chia and stir to combine.

Warm the tortilla or flatbread (to prevent cracking) and then spread the bean paste in the middle of your tortilla. Slice long, thin strips of the vegetables of your choice from the list above. Lay in layers on top of the bean paste.

Last, top with spinach leaves, romaine, or garden greens. Fold the tortilla over and you're ready to pack for lunch or serve. The wraps can be held in place by toothpicks, or secured in waxed paper to make an easy take-along.

Vegetable Options

cucumber slices

carrots, thinly sliced

roasted red pepper strips

tomato, thinly sliced

spinach, romaine, or other greens

Dry Ingredients

1 can (14.5 oz) cannellini beans

2 cloves of garlic

1 teaspoon ground cumin

½ teaspoon red pepper flakes

6 tortillas

1 tablespoon dry chia seeds

Wet Ingredients

3 oz non fat/low fat cream cheese

juice of 1 lemon

Do you have leftover rotisserie chicken? These easy wraps make a great dinner for two when served with a side dish. This dressing is light, so it lets the flavors of the vegetables and chicken shine through. The cumin spices up the light sour cream, so there's no need for mayo. Extra wrap? Pack it for an easy lunch the next day. This recipe makes two large wraps.

Creamy Avocado Chia Wrap

DIRECTIONS:

In a bowl, smash the avocado with a fork to make a paste. Add the sour cream, cumin, vinegar, and chia gel. Add the remaining chopped veggies and the chicken and fold to coat. Warm the wraps in the microwave for about 8 seconds to prevent cracking while folding. Place your greens in the center of the wrap and spoon on the chicken salad. We like to fold our wraps into wax paper so that eating them is less messy. They're perfectly portable this way for a grab-'n'-go lunch, too.

1 cup shredded cooked chicken

½ ripe avocado

1 large plum tomato

½ cucumber, peeled, de-seeded, and chopped

1 ring red onion, chopped

½ green apple

fresh parsley to taste

⅓ cup light sour cream

½ teaspoon cumin

1 teaspoon white wine vinegar

1 tablespoon of chia gel

greens of choice

The "Just a Little Kick" Southwestern Chia Dressing (see page 149) in this quick assembly sandwich is tastier and less caloric than mayo. Eat over a plate, as this is messy but delicious. Makes two sandwiches.

Tuna Avocado Spread

DIRECTIONS:

This spread is super easy to make. Just open
your tuna and drain. Place into a small bowl and
add the "Just a Little Kick" Southwestern Chia
Dressing and stir to combine. Dice the celery and
mix it in. Slice the avocado and tomato. Spread the
tuna on your bread of choice, top with the tomato,
avocado, and greens and you're ready to go.

1 can of tuna

2 tablespoons "Just a Little Kick"
Southwestern Chia Dressing

1 large tomato slice diced celery
avocado slices
salad greens of choice

4 slices bread or 2 bagel-thins
or rolls

Tip: If you're using a bagel, just add a second leaf for the bottom to cover the hole.

Try this chia twist on trendy panini sandwiches! You'll love the sun-dried tomato topping—and the fact that these aren't loaded with butter. You can easily make them in a skillet, countertop grill, or panini machine. Any way you do it, these make a fantastic lunch or dinner! This makes two sandwiches.

Light 'n' Easy Chia Panini

DIRECTIONS:

First, add the sun-dried tomato slices to the food processor and pour in the 2 tablespoons of very hot water. This will re-hydrate the tomato pieces so they become easy to process and spread, but they'll still retain that distinctive sun-dried taste.

Let this mixture stand while you cook the chicken breast. Then, simply add all the ingredients except the bread, chicken, cheese, and coleslaw mix to the food processor. Mix until the ingredients form a chunky red paste.

Thoroughly cook the chicken breast in the microwave. Then, cut into thin slices and set aside. You can also cook the chicken in your countertop grill, if you prefer.

Slice your bread of choice and toast it either in a toaster or on your grill. Once the bread is toasted and crisp, spread the mixture onto the top and bottom. Lay in the chicken breast slices and layer on the shredded coleslaw mixture. If you want, add a thin deli slice of provolone cheese and top with the other bread slice.

To cook the sandwiches for the great panini taste, spray your skillet (or panini machine) with cooking spray. Also spray the outside of the breads as well to prevent sticking. Place sandwich in grill or skillet set to high heat, and press down for about 2 minutes or until toasty and the cheese has melted.

Dry Ingredients

4 slices bread of your choice
¼ cup sun-dried tomato pieces
1 teaspoon oregano
1 clove garlic
¼ teaspoon black pepper
1 chicken breast
⅓ cup shredded coleslaw mix
2 Provolone cheese slices

Wet Ingredients

1 tablespoon balsamic vinegar
¼ cup roasted red pepper slices
2 tablespoons boiling water
1 teaspoon chia

Tip: Select a sturdy, dense, or thick bread; thin slices from ordinary loaves can break apart during the panini-making process. Ciabatta bread is shown here; it's the most commonly selected for paninis.

If you don't have a panini machine: These will still turn out tasty in a counter top grill; just press down on the lid while it cooks. To prepare in a skillet, use another smaller skillet to press down on the sandwiches as they toast.

Chia
Dinners

With our busy lives, getting the family together for dinner can be a challenge. It helps if you have delicious, colorful, and easy-to-prepare food!

None of these dinners require long stove-top or oven cooking times. If something is too difficult, or not worth it's while, it will be left off the menu—no matter how good it is for you. Included in this section are make-ahead dinners, dinners that can provide you with leftovers to eat for lunch the next day and simple soups that can be a whole dinner or a side. These use fresh, tasty ingredients that should be available to almost anyone. You'll find great tastes for vegetarians and omnivores alike. Some of the dishes are meat-optional, so you can decide which, if any, meat to use.

The chia in these recipes is mostly used as an added health ingredient. These recipes illustrate how easy chia is to incorporate into delicious healthy meals. When you eat food with chia mixed in, it keeps you feeling full longer than normal. This is helpful for anyone trying to lose weight, or avoid second helpings. For many of the recipes, you can add more chia than the amount indicated in the ingredients if you want more fullness-power. The chia also adds two kinds of fiber, healthy omega-3 oil, and B vitamins.

The other way chia is used is as a flavor-combiner in many of the soups, sauces, and dressings. When chia hydrates in ingredients or chia gel is added, it can help blend flavors together for a better overall taste.

Fast, fun dinners can help bring the family together before mealtime, as well. "Cooking helps you appreciate and enjoy your food more, especially if you share the process with others," says Michael Pollan, author of *The Omnivore's Dilemma*. He also says that "people who cook tend to eat more healthfully and weigh less than those who don't."

See how much fun shaking up your menu can be! Try one of these recipes for tonight's dinner.

Put the jar of pasta sauce back on the shelf when you're ready to try this fresh, light pasta dish. Pull out your best chopping knife and your veggies and become a kitchen whiz kid. Now you can add to your five servings of fresh veggies in a tasty way. Freshly made fast and easy sauce with great spices and loads of veggies really makes a difference here. It's not nearly as heavy as the canned variety, and you'll get more nutrients, too. This recipe makes two to three servings.

Garden Chia Pasta

DIRECTIONS:

First prepare the tomato, onion, carrot, celery, and garlic. Begin boiling the pasta according to package directions.

While the pasta is cooking, you can brown and crumble the meat of choice in a skillet. When done, drain the grease away from the meat and move to a small plate.

While spaghetti is boiling, add the olive oil to the same skillet you used for the meat. Sauté the onion and garlic until slightly tender. Add the oregano, basil, and chia with the tomato paste and a little of the pasta water (about $\frac{1}{3}$ cup) to make a light tomato sauce. Toss in the tomato, shredded carrot, zucchini, and celery in the skillet and fold to combine, warming the vegetables just slightly. Stir in the meat. Drain the pasta and plate your garden medley.

1 large tomato, de-seeded and diced

½ zucchini, peeled and chopped

¼ pound ground sirloin or ground turkey

¼ large white onion, diced

1 large carrot, grated into large shavings

1 stalk of celery, chopped

2 cloves of garlic, smashed and finely diced

1 tablespoon of dried basil

1 tablespoon of dried oregano

1 tablespoon of dry chia

small handful of chopped flat-leaf parsley

4 tablespoons of tomato paste

2 tablespoons of olive oil

⅛ teaspoon dried pepper flakes

grated Parmesan-Romano cheese

whole-wheat spaghetti for 2–3 servings

This is a grown-up take on homemade cheesy-mac, but don't be surprised if kids love it, too! It has colorful veggies, panko bread crumbs, and even brings a little heat! You'll love the various cheeses that give this meal its great texture, and the chia seeds help fill you up so that one serving is plenty. Serves four to six.

Grown-Up Macaroni and Cheese Dinner

DIRECTIONS:

First, cook the pasta according to package directions. As you are waiting for it to cook, you can shred the cheddar cheese. Set aside ½ cup shredded cheese to sprinkle over the top before you bake it.

Cut the carrot into bite-sized rounds, and slice the celery stalk. Mince the garlic clove. In a bowl, combine the sour cream, cottage cheese, 1 ½ cups shredded cheddar/pepper jack, vegetable pieces, and minced garlic. Then, add the hot sauce, pepper flakes, parsley, and chia. Stir to combine.

Drain the pasta, and stir it in. Once everything is well combined, transfer the mixture into your 8 x 8 baking dish. Sprinkle the reserved ½ cup shredded cheddar cheese over the top, and then sprinkle on the panko bread crumbs.

Bake at 350 for 10 minutes. Then turn the oven to "broiler" and broil for 1 minute to brown the top and crisp the bread crumbs. Let it rest for about 5 minutes before serving.

The heat in this dish depends on what brand of hot sauce you choose. Make this as hot or as mild as you like!

Dry Ingredients

2 cups penne pasta

1 cup shredded sharp cheddar cheese

1 cup shredded pepper jack cheese

1 celery stalk

1 clove garlic

1 handful fresh parsley

1 medium carrot

¼ cup parmesan cheese

3 tablespoons panko bread crumbs

1 tablespoon dry chia seeds

½ teaspoon red pepper flakes

Wet Ingredients

1½ cups low fat cottage cheese

½ cup light sour cream

a couple of drops of hot sauce of your choice

A taste of the tropics…any time of the year! If you're looking for a pick-me-up energy-boosting salad, try this one. It's best with kiwi in it, but if they are not in season, you can make it, anyway. This salad has everything you need for lasting energy: protein (shrimp/chicken and chia), natural sugars, vitamin C from the fruit, carbohydrates for lasting energy (pasta shells), and leafy greens for health and vitamins. It is a powerhouse of flavor and energy! This recipe makes two servings.

Tropical Sunshine Shrimp Salad

DIRECTIONS:

Cook the pasta according to package directions. While the pasta is boiling, peel and slice the kiwis. Mandarin oranges can either be sectioned when fresh, or if they are out of season you can get them canned or in those little plastic cups. Wash and cut the zucchini.

Rinse and drain the pasta shells. In a large bowl, place the fruits, zucchini, chicken or shrimp, and pasta.

You can mix the dressing in a measuring cup. Stir together the sour cream, yogurt, orange juice concentrate, zest, and dry chia seeds. Mix well. Pour the dressing over the salad ingredients to coat. The seeds will cling among the ingredients to help you feel full. If you like, you can add your favorite nut as a topping. Cashews or pecans will work well, and they add healthy nut oils as well as crunch.

Place your choice of greens on the plate and spoon the salad over the top. This may be served now, but will taste best if covered and refrigerated for a few hours.

8 oz. of shredded cooked chicken OR precooked shrimp

2 sliced kiwis (or 1 cup of seedless grapes)

½ cup dry pasta shells

2 4-oz cups of mandarin orange sections OR 2 sectioned mandarin oranges

1 small zucchini cut into match-stick pieces

1 tablespoon dry chia

2 big handfuls of your favorite greens

Dressing Ingredients

1 tablespoon low fat sour cream

1 tablespoon low fat plain yogurt

2 teaspoons orange juice concentrate

1 teaspoon fresh orange zest

Think you can't fill up with "just a salad"? Try this great new take on the Waldorf salad and you may change your mind. When you include fruits, vegetables, beans, grains, and seeds every bite is packed with flavor and nutrients. The lentils, bulgur, and chia make it filling, but the fresh grapes, leafy greens, and lemony tang keep it light and unique. No need for mayo!

New Waldorf Chia Salad

DIRECTIONS:

First, cook the bulgur wheat according to package directions in the 1¼ cup water with 2 tablespoons lemon juice. This infuses the bulgur with great flavor. When the bulgur is nearly cooked, remove from heat and stir in the chia seeds.

You can use canned lentils, or cook dry lentils according to package directions. Use your favorite color of lentils. Canned lentils save time, and beans keep a high percentage of their nutrients despite the canning process.

While the bulgur is cooking, cut all the grapes into halves, and chop up the apple. Mince the garlic, zest the lemon, and dice the red onion.

Once the bulgur and lentils are ready, mix them together. Lay down a bed of garden greens or baby spinach on the plates or in the bowls. In a medium bowl, combine the chopped apple, cut grapes, and parsley. In a measuring cup, mix the minced garlic, lemon zest, basil, lemon juice, olive oil, and onion. Pour this mixture over the fruits in the bowl and stir gently to coat, and then add the bulgur and lentil mixture. Stir again to coat.

Place the mixture over the greens, then select your desired topping from the list and you're ready to serve.

- 1 cup seedless white grapes
- 1 red apple
- ½ cup lentils
- ½ cup bulgur wheat
- 1 tablespoon dry chia seeds
- 1¼ cup water
- 2 tablespoons lemon juice
- 1 cup baby spinach OR garden greens
- ½ cup fresh parsley
- zest of 2 lemons
- ½ teaspoon fresh basil
- 2 tablespoons red onion
- 1 clove garlic
- 1 tablespoon lemon juice (for dressing)
- 1 tablespoon olive oil

{ Add crunch without croutons! Try mixing it up by choosing 1 or 2 of these optional toppings. You'll get crunch without the carbs.
- walnut pieces
- chopped pecans
- small crumble feta cheese
- sunflower seeds
}

Here's a delicious meat-free dinner that's colorful and flavorful. Cheese raviolis are used here, but spinach ones will work as well. This garlicky meal is so easy because it can be made all in one pot. If you can chop veggies and follow package instructions, you can make this delicious, easy meal. This recipe makes two servings, but it can easily double.

Chia Ravioli One Pot Dinner

DIRECTIONS:

First, prepare the vegetables by chopping the cauliflower, broccoli, and zucchini into bite-size pieces. Cut the carrot into thin rounds.

Next, cook the ravioli according to package directions. Once they're cooked, drain and remove the ravioli. To that same pot, add the olive oil and minced garlic. Turn down the heat on the stove and brown the garlic. Once the garlic has browned, return the ravioli to the pot.

Sun-dried tomatoes usually come in sealed bags as chunks. Slice these into small strips, as they pack big flavor—you'll want it evenly distributed throughout each plate of food.

Dry Ingredients

1 13-oz package cheese ravioli
½ cup broccoli
½ cup cauliflower
½ cup carrot rounds
½ cup zucchini, chopped
½ cup sun-dried tomato, julienned
2 deli slices provolone, in strips
1 bunch arugula or spinach

Wet Ingredients

1 ½ tablespoons olive oil
2–3 cloves garlic cloves (minced)
2 tablespoons chia gel

Lower the heat, then add all the chopped vegetables and stir to coat. Last, add the arugula or spinach and stir lightly just until wilted. Add the chia gel—it will cling to the ingredients as you stir.

Spoon onto plates and cut the provolone into strips. Place the strips on top and you're ready to serve this easy colorful one-pot meal.

{ Did you know…?
Garlic may be blamed for bad breath, but it can also claim some credit for better health. It is a natural antibiotic, and salmonella bacteria die when it is present. It's also an antioxidant, which means it fights free radicals that can cause aging damage in the body. The more you chop or crush garlic, the more benefits it provides. Garlic contains allicin, which prevents the oxidization of LDL cholesterol—and that's good news for your arteries! }

With or without meat, this dish is colorful, hearty, and fresh. The chicken breast cubes here are optional, but with the crunchy nuts, chia, and bulgur wheat, this dinner will always be filling. Add your choice of greens as the base. This recipe makes two servings.

Peach and Bulgur Chia Crunch Dinner

DIRECTIONS:

First, cook the bulgur wheat according to package directions, using the water and the orange juice concentrate to flavor it. Then, cut the peach into bite-size pieces and slice both stalks of celery on the bias to create interesting shapes. Chop the red onion and the parsley.

In a large bowl, combine the chopped fruit and vegetables with the cooked bulgur wheat. Add the white balsamic vinegar, 1 tablespoon dry chia, and the orange zest. Stir to combine and thoroughly coat all the ingredients. Be sure to use white vinegar, as dark balsamic vinegar will turn the dish brown. The chia will cling to the ingredients and seasonings.

Place 1 cup of mixed garden greens on each plate. Scoop the mixture onto the greens. For added crunch, you can use ⅛ cup of nuts of your choice.

With so many great flavors, no one will miss the meat. However, if you'd like to add extra protein you can easily make chicken breast cubes to go with the meal. (Or chop the chicken breast into medallions and stir it in when you're mixing in the vegetables.)

To prepare the chicken, divide the chicken breast in half, then cut at an angle to create the medallion shape. Then, season with salt and freshly ground black pepper. Cook in the microwave or in the oven until no longer pink inside.

Dry Ingredients
1 peach OR nectarine
½ cup uncooked bulgur wheat
2 stalks celery
1 large handful curly parsley
2 tablespoons chopped red onion
¼ cup nuts
2 cups wild garden greens (your choice)
1 chicken breast (if desired)
1 tablespoon chia
1 teaspoon orange zest

Wet Ingredients
1½ tablespoons white balsamic vinegar
1 tablespoon orange juice concentrate
1¼ cups water

Tip:
This dish works best with fresh fruit. If peaches AND nectarines are out of season, you can use fresh figs. Dried figs are a little chewy and may make it too sweet for you. If you don't like nuts, you can sprinkle toasted sunflower seeds instead to get the crunch.

We are all busy and sometimes there is just no time to cook. This chili is so quick to prepare, and there is just about nothing to it. If you have a pot and a can opener, you can have delicious chili in much less time than you'd think. Just go to your pantry and fridge and pull out the ingredients. If you like your chili really hot, add a little jalapeño pepper to suit your palate. This recipe makes about four servings.

4-Can Speedy Chia Chili

DIRECTIONS:

In a large saucepan, brown the meat and drain the grease away. Leave the meat in the pan. Return the saucepan back to the stove and add all of the remaining ingredients. Let this simmer for about 10 minutes. Incredibly, that's all there is to it!

1 pound ground beef/chicken/turkey

1 clove minced garlic

1 can drained sweet corn

1 can kidney or red beans, rinsed and drained

1 can chunky tomatoes

1 4-oz can diced green chilies

½ teaspoon dried basil

1 tablespoon of chili powder

2 tablespoons gelled chia

½ teaspoon red pepper flakes

This quick and easy taco salad can be your go-to dinner when you want good "fast food." Feel free to add a little of your favorite hot sauce to the meat mixture to crank up the heat. We like it just as printed, so taste the sauce first and then adjust it if you desire. If you want to prepare an edible taco bowl for the fun of it, the directions are at bottom of the recipe. This makes four dinner salads.

Quick Chia Taco Salad

DIRECTIONS:

In a skillet, brown and drain the fat from the ground meat. Lower the heat and add the ketchup, chia gel, cumin, and chili powder and stir.

Place the lettuce greens on four plates and evenly divide the meat mixture, tomatoes, avocados, etc. Top with shredded cheese and the dressing.

How to make an edible bowl:

Warm 4 tortilla shells in the microwave for 20 seconds. Spray both sides of each with cooking spray. Place over an inverted empty, clean coffee can or other large container. Lightly shape the way you want them to drape. Bake at 425 degrees for about 10 minutes on a baking sheet. Once lightly browned, remove from the oven and let the bowls cool so that they become firm.

These bowls can be made earlier in the day and stored in an airtight container until fiesta time.

1 pound ground beef, chicken, OR turkey

2 chopped rings of a large red onion

$1/3$ cup ketchup

2 tablespoons of chia gel

2 teaspoons chili powder

1 teaspoon ground cumin

6 handfuls salad greens of your choice

2 chopped tomatoes

1 thinly sliced avocado

6 sliced black olives

$1/4$ cup grated sharp cheddar cheese

"Just a Little Kick" dressing (see page 149)

tortilla chips or rounds to make the "bowls"

This dinner is the speedy key to some great make-at-home Chinese food. The ramen noodles cook quickly and the sweet potato is pre-cooked in the microwave so you're not standing over the stove. The ginger and pepper flakes give this the characteristic heat of Szechwan dishes. Makes about four servings.

15 Minute Chia "Szechwan" Stir-Fry

DIRECTIONS:

Pierce the sweet potato skin with a fork in multiple places. Place in microwave and cook on high for approximately 3 ½ minutes. The potato should still be firm in the center. While the potato is cooking, assemble all the ingredients.

In a 2 quart saucepan, start the water boiling for the ramen noodles.

Heat your wok or skillet and swirl in the oil. Let it heat until a few drops of water will sizzle when flicked into the pan.

1 medium sweet potato

1 small package snow peas

$^1/_3$ cup broccoli slaw or bean sprouts

handful of fresh spinach

1 teaspoon grated fresh ginger

3 tablespoons soy sauce

2 tablespoons oil

1 chicken breast, OR equivalent of beef, cut into thin strips

1 tablespoon chia gel

1 teaspoon red pepper flakes

2 packages ramen noodles (just the noodles—you won't need the seasoning packets)

Stir-fry the beef or chicken until cooked (usually just a few minutes). Turn down the heat on the stove and add the soy sauce, ginger, red pepper flakes, and chia gel. Stir to coat. Place the snow peas in the wok and roll them to coat and barely cook.

Cut the sweet potato. Do not cut through the skin—you want to be able to pull the skin away from the cubes you have cut and place the cubes in the wok.

Place the noodles in the boiling water and cook for about 3 minutes, or according to package directions.

Place the broccoli slaw or bean sprouts and fresh spinach on top of the wok mixture. Drain the cooked noodles, saving just a tablespoon of the pasta water. Dump the noodles over the wok mixture and roll to coat and wilt the spinach.

Most people know that seafood is good for you. So we were not surprised to find that scallops, in addition to their delectable taste, contain thirteen nutrients that can promote cardiovascular health, plus provide protection against colon cancer. And they are low in calories! This light orange sauce lets the flavors come shining through. Makes two dinner servings.

Citrus Scallops and Veggie Stir-Fry

DIRECTIONS:

This recipe comes together *very* quickly, so have the carrot and spinach prepared first. Cut the peppers into thin slices.

In your stock pot, begin boiling the spaghetti as directed on package.

In a small measuring cup, stir together the orange juice, basil, chia gel, garlic powder, and cornstarch. Set aside.

In the meantime, heat your skillet to hot and swirl in the olive oil to coat the pan. When the oil sizzles when water is flicked into the pan, adjust the heat a little lower and add the scallops. Brown the scallops for about 1 ½ minutes and then turn and brown them for another 1 ½ minutes. Don't move them around the skillet very much as they may begin to fall apart. Avoid over-cooking scallops because they will become tough and chewy. Remove pan from heat and scallops from pan into a small bowl. The scallops will continue to cook when set aside.

Return the skillet to the heat. Pour in the orange juice mixture. Add the carrots, peppers, spinach, and scallops to the pan.

Cook about 1 minute or until the spinach begins to wilt. If sauce becomes too thick, add a little water. Add the drained pasta and toss.

3 ounces uncooked spaghetti, broken in half

½ pound fresh scallops

2 tablespoons orange juice concentrate with 5 tablespoons filtered water (or ½ cup orange juice)

½ tablespoon cornstarch

½ tablespoon dried basil

$1/8$ teaspoon garlic powder

1 tablespoon chia gel

1 or 2 tablespoons olive oil

½ each of a red and orange sweet pepper

1 large carrot sliced on the bias

2 cups torn fresh spinach

Our Cuban friend introduced us to picadillo ("pic-a-dee-yo"). When she told us the recipe included olives and raisins, we had our doubts, but it turns out to be delicious and easy. It's not chili, it's not spaghetti, but it's hearty, meaty, and unique. Makes two servings.

Almost Cuban Chia Picadillo

DIRECTIONS:

Spray a large skillet with cooking spray and add the ground meat. Break up and brown the meat and then drain off any fat.

Add the diced tomatoes, garlic, onion, peppers, raisins, and olives. Stir to combine. Now add the cumin, chili powder, and dry chia. Simmer for 15–20 minutes.

While the picadillo is simmering, make your rice according to standard directions. If you want, add a teaspoon of dry chia to the rice and add an additional ⅛ cup water.

½ pound ground turkey or ground beef

⅛ cup raisins

¼ cup green olives

½ cup chopped green, red, or yellow sweet peppers (frozen works well)

1 14-oz can diced tomatoes

½ small red onion, chopped

2 cloves minced garlic

1 tablespoon cumin

1 teaspoon chili powder

1 tablespoon dry chia

½ cup rice

1 cup water

Curry night is always a favorite of ours. The passing of all the condiments makes a lively, festive meal. Curry is the generic name of a mixture of commonly used spices in Asian cuisine. Most recipes and producers of curry powder include coriander, turmeric, cumin, nutmeg, and red pepper in their blends. You can make the sauce as mild or hot as you like. There are many blends of curry powder, so find one that suits your family's palate. This makes two dinner size servings.

Chia Curry

1 chicken breast cut into bite-size pieces

¼ cup diced onion

1 tablespoon olive oil

⅓ cup milk (dairy, almond, coconut, etc.)

½ large red apple, chopped

¼ cup raisins

½ tablespoon curry powder

2 tablespoons chia gel

½ cup rice

1 cup water

Condiments, chopped: tomato, cucumber, banana, nuts, and coconut shreds

DIRECTIONS:

Chop the chicken breast, onion, apple, and condiments.

Start simmering the rice in the cup of water.

Saute the chicken pieces and onion in the olive oil until the chicken is no longer pink in the middle. Remove the skillet from the heat and move the chicken to the sides of the skillet. Pour in the milk and chia gel into the space provided and add the curry powder. Mix to distribute the powder into the milk. Turn the heat down to very low and put the skillet back on the burner. Add the chopped apple and raisins and stir to combine. Taste the sauce. Add a little more curry if you like, but bare in mind that the curry powder will bloom and become hotter. Keep the mixture warm but don't let the milk curdle.

Check the rice. Once the rice is done, plate the rice and top with the curried chicken mixture. You may want to either pass the prepared condiments in small bowls at the dinner table or, if you know what your family likes, divide the condiments evenly and place on the top.

This satisfying supper is great in the winter months. Over-stuffed potatoes can be meatless or made with leftover beef. It is so hearty that you won't miss the meat if you choose to skip it. Russet or sweet potatoes are both delicious stuffed. Makes two servings.

Over-Stuffed Chia Potatoes

DIRECTIONS:

Begin by microwaving your potatoes. White baking potatoes take longer to cook than sweet potatoes, so please bare that in mind as you prepare the rest.

In a small skillet that has been sprayed with cooking spray, sauté the beef with the minced garlic. Lower the heat and add the ketchup, dry soup mix, vinegar, mustard, chia, and chipotle powder. The sauce will be too thick, so add a little water to thin it and lower the heat even more. Put the remainder of the vegetables in the skillet and coat with the sauce.

Let the mixture warm until the potatoes have cooked. Before serving, cut the potatoes lengthwise and use a fork to break up the interior so that it will be easier to eat. Place a serving of the vegetable sauce over the potato and enjoy.

2 baking potatoes, approximately the same size, scrubbed, and pierced with a fork in several places

½ cup canned red beans, rinsed and drained

thinly cut beef pieces (optional)

1 tomato, chopped

1 ear of corn, kernels removed, OR ½ cup canned or frozen corn

small handful of flat left parsley

½ zucchini cut into large chunks

1 small sweet pepper, chopped

2 cloves garlic, minced

For the sauce:

½ envelope dry onion soup mix

1/3 cup ketchup with about 3 tablespoons water to thin it

2 tablespoons white vinegar

1 tablespoon yellow mustard

dash of dry chipotle powder OR chili powder

1 teaspoon dry chia seeds

Need a quick dinner? This is our go-to pesto when there is a time crunch. We can make a batch in the mini-chopper and use it for this dinner and then finish the leftovers on burgers with mozzarella a few days later. Makes two dinners.

Presto Pesto and Chicken

DIRECTIONS:

First, boil the pasta, ravioli, or tortellini according to package directions. While the pasta is boiling, place all the ingredients for the pesto into your mini chopper and pulse until finely cut and blended.

In a small skillet, heat the shredded chicken, broth, and sliced olives. Stir in the amount of pesto you will require to "dress" your pasta. Thin again if necessary with broth. Drain the pasta. Plate the pasta, dress with the chicken pesto, and garnish with tomato wedges and a little parmesan cheese on top.

Ingredients for spinach chia pesto

2 large handfuls of fresh spinach

¼ cup fresh basil OR ⅛ cup dried basil

2 tablespoons parmesan cheese

½ tablespoon olive oil

1 large clove garlic

¼ cup low-salt chicken broth (or vegetable broth)

1 teaspoon dry chia seeds

Ingredients for dinner

1½ cups dry bowtie pasta OR cheese ravioli/tortellini

1 chicken breast, thoroughly cooked and shredded, OR leftover rotisserie chicken, shredded

⅓ cup black olives

1 tomato cut into thin wedges

Additional broth

Your crowd will go wild for this tasty rice. This festive dish is a little bit crunchy, a little bit sweet, and very flavorful. It's suitable as a side dish for anyone, from omnivores to vegans, and it's also very easy to make. With so many great flavors, no one will miss the meat. However, if you'd like to add extra protein, you can easily make chicken breast medallions to go with the meal. To prepare the chicken, divide the chicken breast in half, then cut at an angle to create the medallion shape. Then, season with fresh ground/cracked black pepper. Cook in the microwave until no longer pink inside. Makes four dinner servings.

Rice Goes Wild!

DIRECTIONS:

First, cook the rice in the vegetable broth and water according to package directions *only* until it is slightly undercooked. If the rice came with a seasoning packet, discard it. While the rice is cooking, you can prepare the vegetables. Chop the celery and cut the baby carrots into match sticks. When the rice has absorbed a majority of the liquid, stir in the thyme and chia.

While the rice cools, use kitchen shears or a knife and cut each prune into quarters. Chop the parsley coarsely, leaving whole leaves and removing all stems.

Put the prunes, cranberries, celery, parsley, and carrot sticks into a large bowl. Rinse and drain the chickpeas, and add them to the bowl, too.

This is served medium-warm or cold. Put the cooled rice in the bowl with the other ingredients and mix to combine. You're ready to serve!

1 package of wild/white rice mix
2 stalks celery
12 pitted prunes
1/3 cup dried cranberries
1 handful flat leaf parsley
12 baby carrots
1 cup chickpeas / garbanzo beans
2 tablespoons dry chia
½ tablespoons ground thyme
1 can (14 oz) vegetable broth
½ cup filtered water

{ Wild rice is a whole grain. It has lots of healthy fiber and more protein than wheat. Did you know that wild rice also has B vitamins and magnesium? With wild rice, dried plums, chia seeds and garbanzo beans, this dinner has a fantastic fiber content to enhance digestion. }

Sweet and hot—from the tropical pineapple and the ginger—are a great combination for this easy Oriental dinner. Tropical pineapple is a little sweet and sour, and the ginger adds warm flavor to the dish.

What's the crunch here? The sweet potato! When a sweet potato is almost raw, it has a fun crunch similar to baby carrot sticks. The flavor is mild, different from a cooked sweet potato. Try it! You'll like it.

This recipe makes two to three servings.

Ginger Pineapple Chia Crunch

DIRECTIONS:

First, prepare the rice of your choice according to package directions. While it cooks, cut the chicken breast into bite-size cubes. Sprinkle the cubes with the smoked paprika and set aside. Prepare the vegetables by cutting the raw sweet potato into strips, and cut the white portion of the green onion into small rounds. Chop the celery into bite size pieces.

Grate the fresh ginger root, and cut the cilantro with kitchen shears. Using a skillet or wok, spray the cooking surface with cooking oil spray and stir-fry the chicken pieces. Once thoroughly cooked, add the sweet potato strips, onion, pineapple chunks, and grated ginger. Continue cooking for 3 minutes.

In a measuring cup, add the lemon juice, cayenne pepper, chia, and honey. Add 1 teaspoon corn starch and 2 teaspoons of water and stir. Push the vegetables aside and pour the mixture into the wok or skillet. Stir slowly until the mixture thickens. Once the sauce thickens in the wok, push the vegetables and chicken into it and stir to coat.

1 chicken breast, cubed
½ teaspoon smoked paprika
3 green onions (white portion only)
1 tablespoon fresh grated ginger root
1 tablespoon lemon juice
1 ½ tablespoons cilantro
1 tablespoon sunflower seeds (per plate)
1 pinch cayenne pepper
1 small sweet potato
2 stalks celery
1 cup pineapple chunks
1 tablespoon dry chia
½ cup rice
1 tablespoon honey
½ cup coleslaw mix (per plate)
1 teaspoon corn starch
2 teaspoons filtered water

Plate the rice, then divide the cooked mixture over it. Top this with the coleslaw mix, and add the cilantro on top of that. Sprinkle each plate with the sunflower seeds. If you don't like sunflower seeds, pine nuts will also work well here.

{ Pineapple is healthy and delicious! Not only does it have beta-carotene and B-vitamins, it also has the enzyme bromelian. Bromelian helps digest protein and regulate the body between alkaline and acidic states. It also has anti-inflammatory properties, so pineapple and pineapple juice may be good for a sore throat, too. }

We just love this soup! It's very filling and can be served cool or warm. The sweet potato is high in vitamin B6, beta carotene, vitamin D, and magnesium. It's bright, delicious, and very healthy! Leave the apple skins on the green apples as the whole soup is puréed and you will get all that great fiber. This soup has a little kick to it. This makes about four small bowls of soup.

Creamy Sweet Potato Soup

DIRECTIONS:

Place all of the ingredients (excluding the sour cream and black beans and chia) in a 3 qt. saucepan. Stir to combine the spices into the broth. Bring to a boil and cover, then lower the heat to simmer for about 20 minutes.

Wait for the "almost soup" to cool a little so that you can blend/purée safely. Using a ladle or large cooking spoon, scoop the chunks into the food processor or blender. Be sure not to over purée as the little pieces of veggie add great texture. Stir in the sour cream and add the black beans and chia. We hope there will be enough for your lunch tomorrow!

1 large sweet potato, peeled and cut into chunks

1 green apple, cut into chunks

½ medium-sized onion, cut into chunks

1½ cups vegetable or chicken broth

1 teaspoon grated ginger

½ teaspoon ground cumin

1 teaspoon chili powder

$1/8$ teaspoon cayenne pepper

½ cup light sour cream

1 tablespoon dry chia

½ cup rinsed canned black beans

There is nothing like the aroma of vegetable soup to warm your soul. Vegetable soup can be healthy and tasty, especially when you're not worrying about chemicals in can liners or dealing with over-cooked or over-salted food. When you make this soup, you know exactly what's going into it! This makes six to eight servings. Eat the leftovers for lunch, or freeze to enjoy at a later date.

Spicy Chia Veggie Soup

DIRECTIONS:

In your large "soup pot," sauté the onion in the olive oil. Add the tomatoes, cannellini beans, broth with all the spices, the chia seeds, and vinegar. Stir to incorporate and blend in the chia seeds so that they do not clump. Turn down the heat to low.

In a second, smaller pot, cook the elbows according to package directions until slightly underdone. Drain and add to the soup. Cover and simmer for 20 minutes so that the flavors will infuse.

Just before serving, add in the chopped zucchini and the spinach leaves. Stir gently until the spinach has wilted.

2 tablespoons olive oil

½ red onion, diced

2 (14-oz) cans diced tomatoes

2 cups vegetable broth

1 teaspoon oregano

2 teaspoons chopped fresh basil

1 teaspoon paprika

¼ teaspoon cayenne pepper

2 tablespoons balsamic vinegar

1 tablespoon dry chia

1 can cannellini beans, rinsed

¾ cup cooked elbow macaroni

½ zucchini, peeled and chopped

1 cup torn spinach leaves

This soup is inspired by Chia Fresca, the fresh lime and chia seed drink from Mexico. Sweet potatoes and black beans make it hearty, with or without the meat. It's a unique soup that will help refresh your menu. This makes two large bowls of soup.

Fresh Chia Lime Soup

DIRECTIONS:

You won't spend all day at the hot stove making this soup. It's surprisingly easy and quick. First, use the microwave to cook the sweet potato. Don't cook it all the way through, as it will finish cooking in the soup.

Cut the tomato into bite-size pieces and dice the ¼ jalapeño. If adding chicken, cook thoroughly in the microwave, then cut into bite-size pieces.

In a large pot, add the broth, and bring to a simmer. Stir in the jalapeño, cumin, and squeeze all the juice out of the lime. Sprinkle in the zest. Remove pot from heat and add the tomato. Cut the partially cooked yam into bite-sized pieces and add them to the pot along with the chicken cubes, black beans, and baby spinach leaves. Stir in the dry chia and let stand 5 minutes to help combine the flavors.

¼ of a jalapeño pepper
½ teaspoon cumin
1 sweet potato
⅓ cup black beans (rinsed and drained)
1 teaspoon lime zest (about 1 lime)
1 tablespoon dry chia
½ tomato
1 boneless skinless chicken breast
1 small handful baby spinach leaves
1 tablespoon lime juice (about 1 lime)
14 oz chicken (or vegetable) broth
½ tablespoons light sour cream (garnish)

Divide soup into 2 large bowls and add ½ tablespoon light sour cream to the center of each bowl for a cool garnish. This soup is served only lightly warm, not hot.

The Benefits of Lightly Cooked Food

Over-cooking food has long been known to reduce the nutrients. In some foods the "good stuff" ends up in the cooking water, and in others it can break down the chemicals you needed. This soup is cooked just long enough and not at a high heat. The need for long cooking times and high heat is eliminated by using the microwave for the sweet potato and chicken cubes. Beans are heat resistant, and the tomato actually releases nutrients when heated. The spinach leaves aren't in the heat long enough to do much more than wilt.

Salad Dressings

Have you seen the funny article that claims that the item kept in your refrigerator the longest is bottled salad dressing? The average age is two years! Just think of all the preservatives and additives in those bottles to keep them "fresh" that long. Yikes! It is just a little scary.

A better thought would be to just whisk up a fresh batch of dressing as needed. All these ingredients are items you most likely stock in your kitchen regularly. So . . . make it fresh! We feel the dressing should not cover up your salad, but enhance the flavors of your salad choices.

When you make these simple, fresh dressings you know exactly what's going into them. No artificial dyes, preservatives, or artificial flavors. There are great unique tastes acquired from fresh fruits and herbs here that you just can't get out of a bottle. Most of these can literally be mixed up in under five minutes. You'll also see some tasty salad suggestions here to match with the dressings. However, you should use these dressings on any salad you really like to serve.

How much dressing do you like to use?

For two salads (tossed) you usually need 4 tablespoons of dressing for full flavor. Hydrated chia works so well as a flavor extender due to the unique property of chia gel. It does not absorb or dilute flavor, but instead distributes it. Because hydrated seeds are mostly water, you are replacing calories and fat with healthy water while *not* losing any of the flavors you crave! Chia even works with store-bought dressings, if you even wanted to consider one after learning about these easy homemade dressings.

If you have a favorite store-bought salad dressing, why don't you try this little calorie saving trick?

The key is to substitute ⅓ of the dressing with chia gel. Stir together and dress the salad as usual. Now the smaller amount of dressing will go just as far, and the salad will taste the same.

Chia won't hydrate in strong acids (lemon juice, vinegar) or in oils (olive oil), but the seeds will still cling among the ingredients.

When you add fruits, nuts, seeds, and vegetables to your salads, you add crunch, colorful variety, and lots of great nutrients, both macro and micro. Keep your salads fresh, interesting, and always in demand as you mix things up with a wide variety of dressings.

If you're watching your calories, try this no-added-sweetener dressing. This uses stevia to bring up the sweetness in the citrus fruits. Its fresh taste can enhance and liven up your favorite greens. The chia helps keep you feeling full even though you only had a side salad. There's a whole tablespoon of dry chia in this dressing. Shake up your taste buds and refresh a salad with this dressing tonight!

Creamy Lemon and Lime Dressing

DIRECTIONS:

In a small bowl, combine zest, juice, honey/
stevia. Whisk in olive oil. Gradually whisk in the
sour cream.

Refrigerate and it will keep fresh for about 2 days.
Makes about ¾ cup dressing.

½ cup light sour cream

zest and juice of 1 lemon and
1 lime

2 teaspoons of honey OR
½ teaspoon stevia

3 tablespoons olive oil

few drops of your favorite
hot sauce

fresh ground pepper

small dash of salt

1 tablespoon dry chia

Make a beautiful spinach and strawberry salad with this dressing! The vivid greens and reds are very appetizing. This makes for a wonderful and unusual side salad any time fresh strawberries are in season. The baby spinach leaves and strawberries make an excellent combination of flavors when tied together with this interesting dressing.

Apple Cider Vinegar & Oil Dressing

DIRECTIONS:

In a small bowl, combine all ingredients and whisk to mix. This will separate if left standing for a minute. Be sure to shake or mix before dressing your salad for best taste.

¼ cup olive oil

2 tablespoons honey OR
½ tsp stevia

2 tablespoons apple cider vinegar

1 tablespoon dry chia

1 dash Worcestershire sauce

1 dash paprika

Lemon and basil are a super combination, while Dijon mustard gives a little kick. Use olive oil on your salad especially if it includes vegetables that contain the fat-soluble nutrients like lycopene, beta carotene, and lutein. These nutrients are absorbed best when eaten with a little bit of healthy fat, just like olive oil.

Lemon Vinaigrette

DIRECTIONS:

Place lemon juice, Dijon, and honey in small container. Slowly pour in the oil, whisking continuously. Makes about ¾ cup.

1 lemon OR 3 tablespoons of lemon juice

1 tablespoon of Dijon mustard

1 teaspoon honey

6 tablespoons olive oil

2 teaspoons dry chia seeds

dash salt

2 tablespoons snipped fresh basil

This is great served with mixed greens with oranges, avocado, kiwi, and/or strawberries. The sweet-tart of the raspberry compliments other fruits well. Salads that use fruits are healthy, colorful, and appealing.

Creamy Raspberry Vinegar Dressing

DIRECTIONS:

Wisk together the ingredients in a small bowl.

¹/₃ cup nonfat yogurt

2 tablespoons raspberry vinegar

1 tablespoon maple syrup OR honey

1 teaspoon dry chia

Raspberry Vinegar

You can buy raspberry vinegar in some supermarkets if they have a specialty vinegar section. However, it may not be available all the time or it could be expensive. Fortunately, this is something you can make for yourself at home! Be sure to use a glass container to store it and it will keep fresh. You'll be surprised at how many different uses you can find for your raspberry vinegar once you make it.

To make raspberry vinegar: Pour ½ cup white vinegar into a small bowl and add ¼ cup raspberries (fresh or frozen). Allow vinegar and berries to steep over night. The following day, use a spoon to smash up the berries in the vinegar to maximize the juice and flavor. Using a sieve, strain the raspberry pulp and pour the vinegar into a clean, lidded glass jar. It's important not to use plastic around strong substances like vinegar, as it can pull chemicals out of the plastic and into your food. You will be surprised how often you reach for your fruited vinegar when making fresh salads.

This dressing is great over fresh spinach and your choice of fruits and veggies. It's so thick, it won't end up on the plate or at the bottom of the bowl. Grilled chicken is a great addition to chef salads. For some crunch, you can sprinkle toasted sunflower seeds on top.

Strawberry Chia Chef Salad Dressing

DIRECTIONS:

In a food processor, pulse the strawberries and the vinegar. Once chopped, add the pepper and chia. This is a *very* thick dressing that clings to all your salad ingredients.

1 cup fresh/frozen strawberries

1 tablespoon red wine vinegar or balsamic vinegar

$1/8$ teaspoon ground pepper

2 teaspoons of dry chia

Like French dressing? Try this fresh variation. It's so easy to make, you won't want bottles of dressing with preservatives and additives hanging around your fridge. Just mix up a batch whenever you're in the mood for salad.

"French Dressing"

DIRECTIONS:

Whisk together all the ingredients in a small bowl to mix, and you're done! Add as much black pepper as you want. Black pepper helps your body absorb nutrients more efficiently in many different foods.

¼ cup olive oil

¼ cup ketchup

3 tablespoons sugar OR equivalent sugar substitute such as stevia or xylitol

3 tablespoons white wine vinegar

1 teaspoon garlic powder

2 teaspoon Worcestershire sauce

dash salt and pepper

1 teaspoon dry chia

Tried the Lemon Chia Vinaigrette? Try this creamy Dijon. Mustard is high in antioxidants and adds lots of flavor while not adding additional calories. Loaded with garlic, this is an aromatic, creamy alternative dressing.

Creamy Yogurt Chia Dijon Dressing

DIRECTIONS:

In a small bowl, stir the ingredients together and let stand for 15 minutes. This standing time will give the garlic a chance to permeate the dressing and the chia a chance to help combine the flavors. Makes about ¾ cup.

½ cup low fat plain yogurt

3 tablespoons Dijon mustard

3 tablespoons lemon juice

1 tablespoon sugar OR honey

1 clove chopped garlic

salt and pepper

2 tablespoons dry chia

We just love this thick "south of the border" dressing, which might remind you of a few Mexican restaurants you've visited. This lighter version dressing/sauce can "pep up" a wrap or sandwich, too. The ingredients are easily doubled.

"Just a Little Kick" Southwestern Chia Dressing

DIRECTIONS:

Simply mix everything together in a small bowl, and you're ready to use. This is excellent if you're having a taco salad or making "edible bowls" (see page 109) for a fun presentation.

¼ cup low fat plain yogurt

¼ cup low fat sour cream

1 small garlic clove finely chopped

2½ tablespoons your favorite chili sauce

squirt of lemon juice

dash of chili powder

1 teaspoon dry chia seeds

The zing of the fresh lime is a nice contrast with a little bit of something sweet. Strawberries and apples pair up well, but so will tiny pieces of diced dates or even grapes. The dressing won't drown out any flavors and always feels light and fresh.

Honey Lime Chia Dressing

DIRECTIONS:

To make this dressing, first stir together the honey and lime juice in a small bowl. Once the honey has completely dissolved, whisk in the oil and chia. Then add the pinch of salt and pepper. This dressing works best when made right before you're ready to serve.

3 tablespoon fresh lime juice
3 tablespoon extra virgin olive oil
1 teaspoon dry chia
1 teaspoon honey
1 pinch salt
1 pinch pepper

Chia

Desserts

Love sweets? Wish you could find some that were better for you? Try some of these great chia desserts. Once you make a few fresh-baked, easy cookies, you won't want to go back to the preservative-filled, dried-up box cookies from the shelf. Hopefully these selections can illustrate how real fruit (and not "fruit-flavored-substitutes") can bring fantastic flavor to your sweets.

Chia is used in these desserts in two basic ways:

Cut the fat—Every time you replace half the butter, oil, or shortening in a recipe with chia gel, you get a dessert with half the fat of the "regular version." As you'll find out though, it still bakes, looks, and tastes the same as the full-fat version.

Add moisture—Cutting the fat can sometimes lead to dry desserts. This isn't something to worry about since chia gel adds moisture. Try the soft, tasty crumb on recipes like the Easiest Carrot Cake (page 171) and you'll see what we mean.

Chia can certainly be used to make dessert time healthier. However, that's not a license to go wild. You can't remove all fat or remove all sugar and still have dessert. That's where the "fills you up faster" property of chia comes in handy. With these deserts, a little goes a longer way.

Dessert Ingredients:

You won't find exotic, expensive flours or specialty shop ingredients in these desserts.

These recipes are meant to be made by anyone, easily. Certainly, if you want to substitute carob chips for the chocolate chips, you can go right ahead, but it's not a requirement.

Love the soft, puffy texture of the classic snickerdoodle? Now you can make them in three different ways! They're delicious sprinkled with cinnamon-sugar, but now you can try cinnamon mini-chip and cinnamon pecan, too. Even though they're half the fat, these still have the light, fluffy snickerdoodle texture you love, and they fill the house with scents of cinnamon as they bake. This makes about fifty cookies.

Chia Snickerdoodles

DIRECTIONS:

In one bowl, combine the flour, salt, and baking powder. Mix well to combine. In a large bowl, use a mixer to cream together the sugar and butter. It should look pale and grainy when done. Next, add the eggs, mixing well after each addition. Then, add the apple sauce and mix again. Lastly, stir in the chia gel by hand.

Gradually add the flour mixture to the butter mixture. A thick dough will form. If the dough feels overly sticky, you can refrigerate it for 15 minutes to make it easier to roll.

You can make 3 different types of cookies or just choose one topping to make for the whole batch. Place the 1 tablespoon cinnamon in a small bowl with 2 teaspoons sugar, and scoop 1 tablespoon of dough onto the mixture. Shake gently, or roll to coat the dough ball in cinnamon-sugar.

Dry Ingredients
2¾ cups flour
2 teaspoons baking powder
1 cup sugar
½ teaspoon salt
1 tablespoon ground cinnamon

Wet Ingredients
9 tablespoons butter or margarine
2 eggs
½ cup unsweetened apple sauce
7 tablespoons gelled chia

Optional Ingredients
mini chocolate chips
chopped pecans

Pecans taste wonderful with cinnamon-sugar on the outside of these cookies. Chop pecans into small pieces to help them stick in the dough. Add the pieces to your cinnamon-sugar bowl.

To make the tasty chocolate version, add mini chocolate chips to your cinnamon-sugar bowl. Only mini chips will work, as they get stuck in the cookie dough easily as it's rolled around in the mixture. The cinnamon and chocolate make a great flavor combination!

Once each cookie is coated, place it on your greased baking sheets. Bake at 350 for about 13 minutes. When done, the edges should be lightly browned, and cookie tops will be firm.

A pie crust with no shortening? A pie that is almost good for you? Gluten-free, too? Now that would be a treat. Try this recipe and you'll be delighted. In a big rush? This also works with a store-bought crust (even the chocolate coating part of the recipe). To make a white chocolate coating, just use white chips instead of chocolate. The tasty chocolate coating for the crust ensures that the crust comes out crisp, never soggy. This makes one pie eight inches in diameter.

Frozen Raspberry Chia Pie

DIRECTIONS:

In a bowl, mix together the above ingredients and pack down so that the juice in the grated apple permeates the oats. Let the mixture rest for about 10 minutes. If the apple wasn't very juicy, you can add 1 teaspoon of extra water to help the ingredients cling to form the crust.

Preheat the oven to 375 degrees. Coat a eight-inch pie pan with cooking spray. Evenly press the oat crust mixture into the pan and up the sides. While the crust is browning, about 15 minutes, you may melt the chocolate chips. In a microwave safe measuring cup melt the chips on high for 33 seconds, stir, and resume melting for 22 seconds. Stir and let cool until pie is out of the oven. Cool crust while you make the filling.

In a deep bowl, using an electric mixer, whip the cream until it is of stiff consistency. Set this aside in the refrigerator. In a bowl, mix together the 2 yogurt cups and the dry vanilla pudding. Use the mixer to completely combine. This mixture will become thick and pasty, but don't worry, the next ingredients will loosen it. Next, using the mixer, add the tablespoon of milk and tablespoon of chia gel. Take ½ cup of the raspberries and smash them with a fork in a small bowl to make raspberry juice and purée. Add it to the pudding mixture and stir with a spoon. If the mixture is still very pasty or seems dry, you can add another tablespoon of milk. Carefully fold in the whipped cream and whole berries.

For the pie crust:

1 small green apple, peeled and grated, equaling ½ cup

1¼ cups rolled oats dash salt

1 teaspoon brown sugar

1 tablespoon vegetable oil

1 tablespoon chia gel

½ cup chocolate chips

For the filling:

1½ cups frozen raspberries, thawed

2 small cups (6 oz) of raspberry low fat yogurt

1 package of vanilla instant pudding

2 tablespoons chia gel

1 tablespoon rice milk OR almond milk

½ cup whipping cream, whipped

Use the back of a spoon to spread the chocolate evenly over the crust.

The pie shell should be cool enough to work with now. Spread the melted chocolate evenly to coat the crust. Use the back of a spoon, and work carefully so as not to lift crumbs from the crust. This makes a "moisture barrier" so that the crust does not become soggy.

Once coated, put the whole chocolate covered crust into the freezer for about 10 minutes. This will solidify the chocolate layer.

Fill the pie crust with the raspberry mixture and freeze. It should solidify in about 4 hours. Before serving, the pie will need to be set out on the kitchen counter to "warm up" just a little so that it can be sliced easily.

{ Why not non-fat or low-fat whipped cream substitutes? They're often loaded with high fructose corn syrup, hydrogenated vegetable oils, corn syrup, and preservatives. Hydrogenated vegetable oils can contain trans-fats, which can raise bad cholesterol. When you look at the package of whipped topping, you'll likely see at least 5 ingredients and up to 18. With whipped cream (that you whip yourself) there's only 1 ingredient. }

So what is a chiffon cake? It combines the lightness of an "angel food" cake with the richness of a butter-based cake. Fantastic! It's an "old fashioned" cake that's not commonly found in restaurants or recipe books. You can't buy it as a box-mix either. If you want to impress guests with a delicious cake they likely won't have tried before, go for this Marbleized Chiffon.

This cake requires an angel food cake pan as the cake "rises" on egg whites, giving you protein without the calories. This looks more complicated than it is, so don't worry—this cake is worth it.

Marbleized Chiffon Cake

DIRECTIONS:

First sift the flour, baking powder, salt, and sugar into a medium bowl. Make a bowl-shaped indentation in the flour to place the egg yolks.

Second, separate the eggs. Crack each egg in a small container (do this because if the yolk breaks and enters into the white, the whites will not beat to a "stiff consistency" later). Pour each white into a large non-plastic bowl. (The whites will whip up high, so the bowl should be larger than average.)

Next, in a 1 cup measuring cup, microwave ¼ cup water for about 30 seconds. Add 2 tablespoons of sugar and the square of unsweetened chocolate. Break up the chocolate with a spoon and stir to combine. Let it sit and melt together while you move onto the next step.

Preheat the oven to 325 degrees. Get out the angel food pan. Important: *Do not grease or spray!*

Next, go back to the large bowl of egg whites. Add the ½ teaspoon of cream of tartar. With an electric mixer set on high, beat until VERY stiff peaks form. You should be able to cut through them with a spatula.

2¼ cup sifted cake flour

1½ cups sugar

3 teaspoons baking powder

1 teaspoon salt

¼ cup vegetable oil

7 eggs separated

¾ cup cold water

¼ cup chia gel

1 teaspoon vanilla

½ teaspoon cream of tartar

Chocolate for batter

¼ cup water

2 tablespoons sugar

1 square (1 oz) baker's unsweetened chocolate

¼ cup filtered water

2 tablespoons sugar

2 tablespoons corn syrup

¼ cup unsweetened cocoa powder

¼ cup semi sweet chocolate chips

Return to the flour and egg yolk bowl. Add the vegetable oil, ¾ cup cold water, and the vanilla. With your electric mixer, beat until smooth.

Slowly pour the flour/egg yolk batter over the stiff egg whites while gently folding to blend. Bring the spatula up from the bottom and over the egg whites. You want to keep all the air you whipped into the egg whites. Fold until the batter is uniform.

Always cut an angel food-type cake with a serrated knife using a sawing motion.

This light, delicious cake can be complimented with a side of fruits like strawberries or raspberries. Want something extra chocolaty? Here is a quick chocolate sauce:

Place all ingredients into a microwave safe measuring cup and microwave for 30 seconds. Stir to combine. Microwave again for about 20 seconds or less, and you're done! If this sits out on the counter top it will solidify somewhat as it cools. To re-liquefy just re-heat slightly in the microwave.

Most ganaches use heavy cream, butter, or oil to help keep the chocolate liquid. This recipe uses only the smaller amount of oil in the chips and has rich cocoa flavor. Use this not only with this cake, but anywhere else you'd like to add a drizzle of chocolate.

Remove ⅓ cup of the batter and add the melted and cooled chocolate you already prepared. Fold again to combine and create the chocolate batter for marbleizing.

Ready? Spoon half of the light batter into the 10" angel food tube pan. Top with half of the chocolate batter in dollops. Pour the rest of the light batter on top. Finally use the last of the chocolate batter to make more dollops. Next, with a knife or narrow spatula, swirl gently through the batters to create the marble effect. Leave definite areas of light and dark batters.

Bake at 325 for about 65 minutes. Cake will spring back when lightly pressed with a finger.

Immediately invert the cake in the pan until cool. Most tube pans come with little "feet" to invert the cake upon. To remove the cake, gently run a knife around the edge and also the center tube. Pull up on the center tube to release the cake. Run the knife carefully under the cake to release the cake from the bottom of the pan. Voila! Your cake!

What is the difference between cake flour and all purpose flour? The protein content. All purpose flour has 11 percent and cake flour has 6 percent. Less gluten/protein provides a lighter cake. This cake only works with cake flour, so substituting is not recommended.

Chocolate chip cookies come in two basic textures, chewy and crispy. This recipe is for the chewiest, most melt-in-your-mouth delicious chocolate chippers you've had. If you like crispy cookies, stay far away because these bake up puffy, light, and never oily. The soft moist cookies are full of big, gooey chocolate chips. They taste fantastic hot from the oven and keep well in sealed containers. However, because they are moist and rich-tasting with no preservatives, they should be refrigerated after a few days to prevent mold. The amount of cookies you'll get depends on the size you choose from the list on page 165.

Ultra Chewy Chia Chocolate Chip Cookies

DIRECTIONS:

First, preheat the oven to 325 degrees and grease your cookie sheets. Mix the melted butter and both sugars until well blended. Then add the vanilla, applesauce, whole egg, and egg yolk. Stir again until thoroughly combined. Last, add in your chia gel and stir again. In another bowl, combine the rest of the dry ingredients except the chocolate chips (flour, baking soda, salt). Once the dry ingredients are mixed, add them slowly to the wet ingredients with a wooden spoon. Stir only until just combined. Last, add in the 2 cups chocolate chips.

Dry Ingredients
2 cups flour
½ heaping teaspoon baking soda
½ teaspoon salt
¼ cup white sugar
1 cup brown sugar
2 cups semi-sweet chocolate chips

Wet Ingredients
8 tablespoons melted butter
4 tablespoons chia gel
¼ cup apple sauce (unsweetened)
1 tablespoon vanilla
1 whole egg
1 egg yolk only

Note: Most cookie recipes only make cookies of a particular size. If you attempt to make the cookies at a size that is not described in the original recipe, you'll run into problems such as undercooking while edges burn, or over-done cookies despite the bake time. These cookies can easily be made in any of three sizes! If you're making large or medium size cookies, you can use jumbo chocolate chips or chocolate chunks. If you're making medium or small cookies, regular-size chocolate chips work best.

For giant cookies, use ¼ cup scoops of dough and bake for about 15 minutes. For medium cookies, use 1½ tablespoon scoops of dough and bake for about 12 minutes. For smaller cookies, use 1½ teaspoon scoops of dough and bake for about 10 minutes.

When done baking, the cookies will become golden brown. The edges may appear lightly toasted but the centers will still be soft and puffy. Be careful not to over bake.

Our friend Florence is a connoisseur of fruit crisps and often is one of our taste testers. She rated this chia fruit crisp as one of her all-time favorites. Let's see if it becomes one of yours, too. You can make this crisp with any seasonal fruit or you can find the frozen varieties at your grocery. Granola helps keep the crisp topping crunchy and the spices in the topping compliment the fruit flavors. The apples add a nice texture to this colorful, easy dessert. This makes one 8 x 8 crisp, usually divided into about nine squares.

Chia Triple Fruit Crisp

DIRECTIONS:

Preheat the oven to 400 degrees. Coat an 8 x 8 baking dish with cooking spray.

In a large saucepan, place the brown sugar, cornstarch, and orange juice and stir until blended. Cook for a few minutes until the sauce has thickened. Add the cinnamon, nutmeg, chia, lemon juice, and dash of ground cloves. Remove from heat and stir in the fruit to coat. Pour the fruit mixture into the prepared baking dish.

In a small bowl, combine the flour and spices. Cut in the butter so that it becomes coarse crumbs. Add the dry oats and granola. Stir to combine. Sprinkle over the fruit mixture.

Bake this treat for about 25 minutes or until the topping is browned. Serve warm and smile.

1½ cups sliced peaches (with or without peels)
1 cup fresh or frozen blueberries
2–3 small green apples, chopped
1 tablespoon lemon juice
¼ cup orange juice

Ingredients for crisp topping:
¼ cup granola
¼ cup quick cooking oats
¼ cup flour
4 tablespoons of cold butter, cut into very small pieces
1 teaspoon cinnamon
½ teaspoon nutmeg

Love strawberries? This is the cake for you! With *two* whole cups of strawberry purée, this cake has a blast of real berry flavor in every bite. You can use fresh or frozen berries, so this cake works in any season. You don't need buttery icing when you use the sweet-tart strawberry drizzle over a warm slice of this very berry bunt cake. This recipe creates a standard 10½ inch bunt cake. When baked, this cake will be light tan in color, with pink strawberry bits throughout, like confetti. Unless food dye is used, it won't come out bright pink.

Chia Super Strawberry Cake

DIRECTIONS:

First, in a medium bowl, sift the cake flour, baking powder, salt, and sugar together. Then, purée enough strawberries to make 1½ cups purée. A food processor, mini chopper, or blender will work well. How many berries are required will depend on the berry size. Once the dry ingredients are sifted together, put all 4 eggs in a small bowl and whisk briskly to beat. Add the chia gel and vegetable oil to the eggs and whisk again.

Pour the wet ingredients into the dry, then pour in the strawberry purée. With a wooden spoon, mix until combined. The cake batter will be fairly thick, and you'll see strawberry pieces within.

Prepare your bundt pan by thoroughly spraying with non-stick cooking oil spray. Depending on the pan, you may want to also dust the interior with flour, to make sure the cake comes out easily. Pour the batter into your bundt pan and bake at 325 degrees for about 45 minutes. When done, cake should spring back when touched lightly.

To make the strawberry drizzle, purée enough strawberries for about ½ cup. Once they're chopped, add the 1 tablespoon of sugar and pulse to combine. Set this aside as the cake bakes and the sugar will extract some of the juice from the purée. To serve, cut slices of the cake and drizzle with the mixture.

Dry Ingredients
3 cups unbleached cake flour
3 teaspoons baking powder
½ teaspoon salt
1¾ cups white sugar

Wet Ingredients
4 eggs
½ cup vegetable oil
¼ cup chia gel
1½ cups strawberry purée

Drizzle Ingredients
½ cup strawberry purée
1 tablespoon sugar OR
¼ teaspoon stevia

{ Why use cake flour? Cake flour has lower protein than regular flour. It's this quality that keeps a cake light and fluffy. It's important to select cake flour for this recipe, as the large quantity of berries would otherwise produce a heavy cake. }

You won't want to bother with store-bought carrot cakes when you see how easy this one is. The warm spices fill the kitchen with a wonderful aroma as it bakes. The non-traditional ingredients make it more moist and richer tasting than anything from a box mix or off of a shelf. Nothing beats real, fresh fruits and vegetables! The cake is sweet enough that you won't feel the need for thick cream cheese frosting, either. This makes one 13 x 9-inch cake.

Easiest Chia Carrot Cake

DIRECTIONS:

Preheat oven to 375 degrees and spray a 9 x 11 or 13 x 9 baking dish with cooking spray.

In a medium bowl, combine the flour, spices, and baking soda.

In a second large bowl, beat the purée, carrots, sugar, crushed pineapple, eggs, and vanilla with an electric mixer until all the ingredients are incorporated. Stir in the chia gel by hand with a spoon.

Add the dry ingredients from your medium bowl to the wet ingredients. Stir to combine. Spread the batter evenly into the pan and bake for 30–35 minutes or until a toothpick comes out clean.

Cool completely on a wire rack and then cut into squares to serve.

2 cups all purpose flour
¾ cup sugar
2 teaspoons ground cinnamon
⅛ teaspoon ground cloves
1½ teaspoons baking soda
dash salt

Wet Ingredients
½ cup crushed pineapple with juice
⅓ cup prune purée
4 medium carrots, grated
(about 4 cups)
2 eggs
3 tablespoons chia gel
2 teaspoons vanilla extract

{ Please don't be frightened, but about a zillion years ago we read an article about prune purée and remembered that it adds richness and sweetness to a recipe, without adding the actual flavor of prunes. When you use prune purée, you need less refined sugar and less oil to get the same great taste and texture. To make prune purée in your food processor/mini chopper, place ¾ cup prunes and ¼ cup very hot water. Pulse until finely chopped into a paste. If need be, add a little more water so that the paste is not too thick. Extra purée? It will keep in an air tight container in the fridge for about two weeks. }

These are an easy treat without the wheat! These cookies don't have any flour at all, but still bake up crisp on the outside, chewy on the inside. They're packed with peanut butter flavor thanks to the use of all natural, unsweetened peanut butter. If a cookie becomes too rich with sugar, it can drown out the taste of the ingredients so all you taste is the sweetness. This is easily avoided here by using unsweetened peanut butter. Want even more nutty goodness? You can mix in whole peanuts or use peanut butter chips. Even though it's only a dash, don't skip the nutmeg. It's very subtle but adds a pleasant complexity to the peanut taste. This makes about forty cookies.

Gluten Free Peanut Butter Cookies

DIRECTIONS:

These cookies are quick, so you can mix them up while you preheat the oven to 350.

First, with an electric mixer, cream the butter and both sugars until a light, grainy texture forms. Next, add the eggs one at a time, mixing after each addition. Then add the vanilla, nutmeg, and baking soda. Stir in the chia by hand. Add the peanut butter and stir again with a large spoon until everything is well combined.

Last, add the oats, 1 cup at a time, along with the chips (or peanuts) of your choice. The batter will become very thick and difficult to stir once you add all of the oats. It can then be scooped onto greased cookie sheets with a cookie scoop or measuring spoon. Ideal cookie size is small, about 2 teaspoons each. They can be placed closely on the sheet, as they don't spread much.

Bake for about 10 minutes. (Be careful not to over-bake! These can dry out.) Cookies are done when edges and bottoms are lightly browned. These will keep well in a covered container for about a week.

Dry Ingredients

3 cups quick cook oats
½ cup white sugar
½ cup brown sugar
1½ teaspoons baking soda
1 dash nutmeg
½ teaspoons salt
1 cup chocolate chips (or peanut butter chips)

Wet Ingredients

2 eggs
1 teaspoon vanilla
2 tablespoons butter (softened)
1 cup all-natural unsweetened peanut butter
2 tablespoons chia seed gel

This is a brown sugar cake recipe, which means the cake will be moist and soft, without being too sweet. Fresh orange zest adds a splash of flavor without affecting the texture. This cake tastes sophisticated and rich, so a little slice will satisfy a chocolate craving. This makes one 9-inch round cake.

This cake doesn't need frosting, but it's super served with fresh, bright orange sauce (page 177).

Sophisticated Chocolate Orange Cake

DIRECTIONS:

First, in a microwave-safe cup or bowl, boil the ½ cup filtered water. Once boiling, carefully stir in the cocoa powder to make a thick pudding-like chocolate mixture. Set this aside to cool as you make the rest.

Next, combine all the dry ingredients in a large bowl, including the chocolate chips, and stir to combine. This step helps prevent the chips from sinking to the bottom once the batter is poured.

Then, whisk together the eggs, butter, vanilla, and chia gel. The mixture will be chunky, as seen in the photo. Next, add the orange zest and mix again. Last, add the chocolate to the egg mixture (it's still quite hot, be careful not to touch it) and whisk to combine.

Add the wet ingredients to the dry in the large bowl and use a large wooden spoon to mix. The batter will be thick. Stir only just enough to combine, being careful not to over-mix.

Pour the batter into a greased cake pan. You can use an 8 x 8 square pan, a 9 inch round pan, or a spring-form pan. Bake at 350 for about 30 minutes. When done, a toothpick inserted in the middle should come out clean.

If serving this with mousse or whipped cream, be sure to wait until the cake is only warm, since hot cakes will melt down any mousse placed on or next to them. The distinctive flavor of this cake will make it one your holiday guests will remember!

Dry Ingredients

7 tablespoons unsweetened cocoa powder

¾ cup flour

1 cup brown sugar, packed

½ teaspoon salt

½ teaspoon baking soda

½ teaspoon baking powder

1 cup chocolate chips or chunks

1 tablespoon finely grated orange zest

Wet Ingredients

2 eggs

½ cup filtered water

5 tablespoons butter

5 tablespoons chia gel

½ teaspoon vanilla

This is a handy and tasty orange sauce. You can thicken it to your desired consistency. Here, it's paired with the Sophisticated Chia Chocolate Orange Cake, but you can use it with all sorts of recipes. Pair it with your favorite vanilla cake or serve with vanilla ice cream. What great uses can you think of for this orange sauce?

Elegant Orange Sauce

DIRECTIONS:

All you need for this recipe is a saucepan on the stove. Combine the sugar and cornstarch, then add the water and boil over medium high heat. The mixture should become clear and thicker. Add the orange juice and concentrate, then bring the mixture back to a boil while stirring. Turn the heat down to a simmer and add the butter. The longer you simmer, the thicker the sauce will become, so simmer until it reaches your desired consistency. Lastly, stir in the orange zest.

½ cup sugar

¼ cup filtered water

juice of 1 orange (about ½ cup)

1 tablespoon cornstarch

$^1/_3$ cup orange juice concentrate

1 tablespoon butter

zest of 1 orange

{ This sauce can be served warm or chilled. It can be spooned over cake or ice cream or used as a classy drizzle on a plate or bowl. This makes about ¾ cup of orange sauce. The sauce will keep in a sealed container in the fridge for about a week. }

We think cupcakes are awesome! They are the perfect portion control—somehow it's easier to eat just one cupcake than just one piece of cake. Light, sunny, lemony cupcakes just bring a smile to your day. We used cake flour here instead of all purpose flour so that the cake is very tender. If you don't have cake flour in your pantry, all purpose flour can be used. (It's the gluten ratio that is the key issue.) This makes about ten large cupcakes.

Oh-So-Lemon Cupcakes

DIRECTIONS:

Preheat the oven to 375 degrees. Prepare your muffin tin with cooking spray. This recipe makes ten large cupcakes.

Sift the flour, baking powder, and salt into a bowl. In another larger bowl, beat the butter and sugar with an electric mixer until light and fluffy. Beat in the eggs one at a time so that each egg is thoroughly incorporated. Mix in the vanilla, chia gel, lemon juice, and ½ of the lemon zest. Gently stir in about a ⅓ of the flour mixture and ⅓ of the milk. Repeat until the flour and milk are incorporated. Do not over mix. (No one likes a tough cupcake!)

Fill the cups about ¾ full and bake for about 17 minutes. (Do the toothpick check as these don't really "brown".) Let the cupcakes rest in the pan for about 10 minutes and then move them to your cooling rack.

Once cooled, you can frost them as shown here with the "Not-so-Sweet Lemon Frosting." Garnish with candied citrus peel, if desired.

1½ cups cake flour
2 teaspoons baking powder
dash salt
⅔ cup sugar
zest from 2 lemons (half the zest for the cupcake batter and half for the frosting)

Wet Ingredients

6 tablespoons butter, softened at room temperature
2 tablespoons chia gel
2 large eggs, room temperature
½ teaspoon vanilla extract
½ cup milk (low fat dairy or almond)
1 teaspoon lemon juice

We think loads of fat and powdered sugar on top of a lovely cupcake smothers the flavor. However, a light, not-so-sweet frosting makes a glorious presentation. With this whipped cream topping, you will need to keep the cupcakes in the fridge if you choose to frost them more than a few minutes before serving. See instructions on page 181.

Not-so-Sweet Lemon Frosting

DIRECTIONS:

½ cup whipping cream

½ cup powdered sugar

2 tablespoons softened low fat cream cheese

1 tablespoon lemon juice

1 teaspoon lemon zest

Beat the whipping cream in a medium bowl with an electric mixer. Beat until the cream becomes stiff. Add the softened cream cheese. Beat again. Next, add the powdered sugar, lemon juice, and zest. Beat to incorporate. Now comes the fun part of the frosting. Scoop the whipped cream mixture into a sturdy plastic bag (such as a zip-top bag). Cut off about ½" of the corner tip of the bag. Now you have your very own disposable pastry bag. Squeeze the whipped cream mixture to the bottom of the bag and twist the top of the bag closed. Give each cup cake a little swirl of frosting.

{ Oftentimes we will frost cupcakes as needed just before serving as the bag of frosting keeps well in the fridge for a few days. }

Looking for a lighter, more chocolatey alternative to banana bread? Try these pretty, swirled chocolate banana bars! Never heavy or dry, this recipe turns out more like a cake. With three whole bananas inside, you won't miss the fruity flavor combining with the fun cocoa swirl! Your guests or family will love eating the golden-brown swirled dessert, and they'll never guess how easy it was to make! Makes one 13 x 9 pan of bars.

Chocolate Chia Banana Swirl Bars

DIRECTIONS:

First, cream the butter and sugar until fluffy. Then, add the egg and vanilla extract and stir until combined. Next, mix in the applesauce, gelled chia seeds, and mashed bananas. It doesn't matter if a few small chunks remain. Ripe bananas (without too many spots) will give the best flavor. This mixture will now be lumpy and yellowish.

Next, combine the dry ingredients and mix together. Add the dry mixture gradually to the wet, stirring well. You'll now have one bowl with all the thick banana batter. Now, scoop out about half of the batter and put it back into the bowl that had your dry ingredients. Add the ¼ cup unsweetened cocoa to half of the batter, and mix until well combined. Banana chips may be visible and this batter will be slightly thicker.

Spread the non-chocolate half evenly into a greased 13 x 9 baking pan. Then, drop spoonfuls of the chocolate batter on top until it is all used. With a knife, drag through the chocolate batter, forming a random swirling pattern on top of the dessert.

Bake at 350 for about 25 minutes. When finished, the edges will become golden brown and a toothpick inserted in the middle should come out clean. Cut into bars or squares, and you're ready to serve!

These moist, delicious bars will keep in a sealed container and do not need to be refrigerated.

Dry Ingredients

¾ cup sugar

1½ cups flour

1 teaspoon baking powder

1 teaspoon baking soda

½ teaspoon salt

¼ cup baking cocoa

Wet Ingredients

4 tablespoons butter

4 tablespoons gelled chia

1 egg

1 teaspoon vanilla

3 medium mashed bananas (about 1½ cups)

½ cup unsweetened applesauce

This is our lowest-fat, easiest, and chocolate-y-est cheesecake ever! It is not a traditional, heavy cheesecake, so don't be expecting that. We've used chia to bind the crust together and to blend the filling together. This 8-inch cheesecake will serve twelve. A small piece is all you need to "tame the chocolate beast," as the chia will help satisfy you.

Cocoa Chia Cheesecake

DIRECTIONS:

In your food processor, place a few graham crackers and pulse until finely chopped. Move to a measuring cup. Repeat the process until you have 1 cup of crushed grahams. Place the graham crumbs in a bowl and toss with the chia gel and melted butter. Once the crumbs are moistened, press the crumbs into the bottom of the spring form pan.

Turn on the oven to 300 degrees.

Wipe out the cracker crumb "dust" from the food processor. Put in the cottage cheese and the 2 eggs. Blend until smooth.

In a large bowl with an electric mixer, beat the cream cheese and sugar until smooth. Add the cottage cheese mixture, cocoa, flour, chia gel, and the vanilla. Beat until smooth and pour into your crust.

Bake for 60–65 minutes. The center of your lovely cake should look set in the middle. Cool on a rack for 20 minutes and then run a thin spatula or knife around the edge of the cheesecake to loosen it. Release the catch on the side of the pan. Continue to cool the cheesecake until a little warmer than room temperature and then wrap it in plastic wrap and chill for at least 4 hours.

To serve this cake to friends, we dusted it with powdered sugar and used a little low fat sour cream for garnish. The second day, we topped the cake with puréed strawberries and a dollop of whipped cream. Both were yummy.

Ingredients for the crust

1 cup finely crushed chocolate graham crackers

2 tablespoons chia gel

2 tablespoons melted butter

Ingredients for the batter

16 oz low fat farmers cheese (OR low fat Neufchatel OR cream cheese)

1 cup low fat cottage cheese

2 eggs

1 cup granulated sugar

½ cup unsweetened cocoa

¼ cup all purpose flour

2 tablespoon chia gel

1 teaspoon vanilla

Can you imagine the aroma of warm apple gingerbread just out of the oven? Your whole house will smell heavenly. This bread-cake is so amazing because it has no shortening, oil, or butter, but is rich and dense. The grated apple has the peel left on so the bread has extra fiber, the chia ups the omega 3s, and with just a little sugar added we would swear that this cake is actually good for you. Apple gingerbread comes together so easily with ingredients you probably already have in the house. The hard part is just waiting for it to bake. Makes one standard size loaf (about 8.5 x 4.5 inches).

Apple Gingerbread

DIRECTIONS:

Spray your loaf pan with cooking spray and turn on the oven to 325 degrees.

In a bowl, stir together all dry ingredients except for the brown sugar.

In a second larger bowl, add the brown sugar, molasses, yogurt, and eggs. Beat or stir until the eggs are incorporated. Stir in the dry ingredients from the first bowl. Next, shred the unpeeled green apple. Fold the apple shreds and chia gel into the batter.

Bake at 325 degrees for 50–60 minutes. Do the toothpick test to check for doneness.

Cover leftover bread with foil. Apple gingerbread tastes great in the morning when slightly warmed and with a smear of whipped, low fat cream cheese.

Dry Ingredients

1 cup all purpose flour
½ cup quick cooking oats
½ teaspoon baking soda
½ teaspoon baking powder
2 teaspoons cinnamon
1 teaspoon ginger
¼ teaspoon nutmeg
¼ teaspoon cloves dash salt
½ cup brown sugar

Wet Ingredients

2 tablespoons molasses
2 tablespoons gelled chia
⅓ cup unflavored yogurt
2 eggs
1 cup shredded green apple

Our friend Steven inherited his diabetes. Whenever he comes to dinner, we are always in a quandary as to what to serve him for dessert besides a cup of sugar-free jell-o or a piece of fruit. We wanted something special that wouldn't harm his blood sugar numbers. So here is our answer to this situation. This sugar-free "cheesecake pudding" and strawberry or blueberry parfait looks festive and has the chia gel in it to help keep his blood sugar steady by slowing down the conversion of carbohydrates into sugars. We are not a proponent of the sugar substitute aspartame and acesulfame potassium, but we figure once in awhile a little can't hurt you. The amount of servings you get out of this recipe will depend on the size and height of your parfait glasses or dishes.

Diabetic Chia Fruit Parfaits

DIRECTIONS:

We have found that having the ingredients all prepared and then assembling the parfait while you make the coffee/tea after dinner works well. If the parfaits are made too early, the ginger snap cookies will absorb the moisture from the pudding.

Prepare the pudding according to the "pie" form (not the pudding form) directions on the package. Add the chia gel and whisk as directed. Cover with plastic wrap and refrigerate. Pulse the cookies in a food processor until they become crumbs. Place in an airtight container.

Prepare the fruit of choice and refrigerate.

Assemble just before you would like to serve by spooning alternating layers of pudding, crumbs, fruit pieces, and nuts. If you don't have parfait glasses, you can serve in a stemmed wine glass.

1 box of sugar-free no cook cheesecake pudding (net wt 1 oz)
1¾ cups low fat milk (use dairy because soy milk will not let the pudding set)
store-bought sugar-free ginger snap cookies, crushed
fresh strawberries or blueberries
2 tablespoons gelled chia
nuts of choice (if desired)

A light, fluffy, melt-in-your-mouth cake for breakfast, tea, or dessert! This cake is so light that you can have it any time of the day, but better hurry because it'll be gone before you know it! The top becomes golden-brown and lightly crisp while the interior is moist without being heavy. Fresh blueberries will taste best, but you can use frozen ones, too. Makes one 8 x 8-inch cake.

Light and Fluffy Chia Blueberry Cake

DIRECTIONS:

First, the eggs must be separated. In a small bowl, beat the egg whites until stiff peaks form. Then, beat in ¼ cup of sugar and set aside. In another bowl, cream the butter with the remaining ¾ cup of sugar, salt, and vanilla. Stir in the egg yolks and then the chia gel. The mixture will be yellow.

Sift flour together with baking powder and add it gradually to the creamed mixture, along with the milk. Once mixed, it's time to fold in the beaten egg whites. Carefully fold in the egg white mixture so the batter becomes smooth and soft.

Prepare the berries: You don't want all the berries ending up on the bottom of the cake! The easy way to prevent this is by coating them in flour. Put 2 tablespoons of flour on a plate, then pour the berries over it. Roll them around until they're all coated.

Carefully fold in the coated blueberries and pour the batter into your greased, 8 x 8 pan. Now it can be topped with cinnamon and sugar, to taste. We use about 1 teaspoon of cinnamon and 2 teaspoons of sugar. Bake at 350 for about 50 minutes. A toothpick inserted into the center will come out clean when done.

We can't imagine there would be much left over but . . . to keep for longer periods of time, it can be stored in the refrigerator or even frozen, then re-heated. It tastes best fresh, of course!

Dry Ingredients

1½ cups flour
¼ teaspoon salt
1 cup sugar
1 teaspoon baking powder
1½ cups fresh blueberries
2 tablespoons flour to coat blueberries

Wet Ingredients

2 eggs (separated)
4 tablespoons butter (best if softened)
4 tablespoons chia gel
1 teaspoon vanilla
⅓ cup milk (low fat)

Topping:

cinnamon and sugar, to taste

Chia

Appetizers and Snacks

Looking for a snack? Or something to take the edge off of hunger before dinner? Try one of these chia snacks or appetizers. Having a healthy snack in the afternoon rather than reaching for a bag of chips or a candy bar can make a real difference in your health and energy levels. Chia adds protein and slows down the conversion of carbohydrates into sugars to provide you with steady, non-jittery energy.

Cutting appetite before a meal can help you eat less.

If you fill up with a chia snack ahead of time, you're less likely to overeat at meal time. Some of these appetizers can even become part of a dinner. There's no rule that says you can't serve vegetables and dip as part of a meal. If you or your family like it and it's healthy, why not?

Poorly chosen snacks can sabotage your healthy eating efforts.

Feeling run down in the afternoon can create a powerful craving for a candy bar. These snacks are meant to help you satisfy a nagging hunger or calm a sweet-tooth without resorting to candy, cookies, or chips. A cracker or veggie stick in garlic-ey dip can give you the quick crunch you were looking for. A chia popsicle can satisfy a sweet tooth with a burst of fruit flavor and wake you up with each cold, refreshing bite. Blood sugar highs and lows can cause cravings and fluctuating energy levels throughout your day. The two kinds of fiber in chia help slow down the conversion of carbohydrates into sugars. This provides you with steady, non jittery energy. By eating chia with a meal you'll use the carbs more slowly. Chia also has complete protein, like that found in meat. (Rare in the plant world!) Protein must always be used right away by the body. It doesn't turn into fat or convert into anything else; it just provides energy.

Chia helps you turn drinks into snacks.

When chia is gelled, it makes your digestive system treat liquids as it would solids. The body has to strip off the soluble fiber from the outside of the seed shell to access the liquid. This helps chia gel stay in the stomach longer, sending out "I'm still full" signals. The insoluble fiber (what you see as the colored part of the seed shell) does not add calories, because it can't be digested at all. It acts as roughage, helping sweep foods along through the digestive system.

In this way, a chia drink, like one of the healthy green teas, can fill you up just like a snack. There are so many different drinks, teas, and fruit juice solutions that you'll never get bored. Add as much or as little chia as you like to control the fullness factor. Want to really knock out hunger? Try a chia sugar free drink about 20 minutes before mealtime. This gives the notoriously slow stomach a chance to start sending fullness signals to the brain before a meal even gets served.

Crunchy toast slices and savory seasoned tomato are a wonderful combination to serve as an appetizer. These tasty slices with great Italian flavor can be served before a meal, or with it. Grandmother used to make a very similar fresh tomato relish when all the plum tomatoes from the garden were ripe at the same time. She would make this as a side dish. We decided that it was so good, we would change very little and make it into a topping for bruschetta. This makes about one cup, depending on the size of your tomatoes.

Plum Tomato Chia Brochette

DIRECTIONS:

In a medium bowl, combine all ingredients and let it stand about 10 minutes. This gives time for the flavors to mingle and the sundried tomatoes to rehydrate slightly.

Place the baguette slices on a cookie sheet and brush with a little additional olive oil. This will help prevent the topping from soaking into the bread. Broil for 1+ minutes until the slices are slightly browned. Remove cookie sheet from oven and divide the relish over the toast. Return to oven to just warm the relish for about a minute. Watch carefully! Remove and sprinkle with the cheese.

This recipe can easily be doubled if you are having lots of guests.

3–4 plum tomatoes, chopped (depending on size)

2 cloves of garlic, minced

$1/8$ cup olive oil

1 tablespoon fresh basil leaves, chopped

1 tablespoon dried basil

$1/4$ cup sun-dried tomatoes, chopped

2 teaspoons balsamic vinegar

1 tablespoon dry chia

$1/2$ baguette, sliced on the bias

Romano/Parmesan cheese to sprinkle on top

Let this be your "go to" recipe for a pesto in a pinch. You can make it in just a few minutes in your food processor and it's so versatile and flavorful. Try it on tortellini or turkey burgers; you can even serve over chicken breast. This tasty pesto is made from fresh spinach and fresh basil. It's bright green, flavorful, and very fresh tasting. The spinach and fresh basil are full of vitamin A, while the olive oil helps with digestion and absorption of vitamins and minerals. Here, the chia helps blend all the flavors together and gives the pesto some added body. This makes a half cup of pesto.

Easy Spinach Chia Pesto

DIRECTIONS:

Easily prepare this pesto by placing the spinach, basil, and garlic in a small food processor with the chopping blade attachment. Chop. Add the olive oil, parmesan, broth, and chia and process the mixture until it forms a thick, fragrant paste.

We love this pesto with a slice of mozzarella cheese on a burger!

1 cup fresh spinach leaves
¼ cup basil leaves or dried basil
2 tablespoons parmesan cheese
½ tablespoon olive oil
1 clove garlic chopped
¼ cup low-salt chicken broth
1 teaspoon dry chia seeds

This no-cook cranberry pomegranate spread is versatile, crisp, and fresh! Delight guests and family when you use it with crackers, chips, cheeses, or on a sandwich! No cooking required, just get out the food processor to make this easy, healthy mix. Everything involved is totally loaded with health benefits. It's bright, cheerful, and sure to impress with fantastic flavor. This makes one small bowl of relish to share.

Cranberry Pomegranate Zippy Chia Relish and Panini

DIRECTIONS:

Rinse the cranberries in a colander. Pick out any under or overripe berries. Rinse the cilantro and shake to dry. Use kitchen scissors to cut off the long stems of the cilantro. Remove the seeds from the pepper.

Put cranberries, cilantro, onion, and pepper in the food processor. Pulse a few times to chop well. Next, add lime juice, agave nectar (or stevia), dry chia and the pomegranate arils. Pulse quickly twice to blend everything together.

It is important to not over-chop or it will become slush. The mixture should be thick and spread-able. For use on crackers, cheese, or chips, just spoon the relish into a festive bowl and you are ready to serve.

½ bag (6 oz) fresh or frozen cranberries

1 handful fresh cilantro

¼ or ⅛ jalapeño pepper, de-seeded

3 tablespoons lime juice

¼ cup pomegranate arils

¼ cup agave nectar OR sweetener of choice (such as stevia)

¼ inch round of a red onion

1 teaspoon dry chia seeds

Panini: Thoroughly cook the chicken breast in the microwave. Then, cut into thin slices and set aside. You can also cook the chicken in your counter-top grill, if you prefer. You can use deli sliced provolone cheese, if you want.

Slice your bread of choice and spread the mixture on top. Lay in the chicken breast slices. If you want, add a thin deli slice of provolone cheese, and top with the other bread slice. To cook, spray your skillet (or panini machine) with cooking oil spray, and spray the outside of the bread as well to prevent sticking. Place sandwich in grill or skillet set to high heat, and press down for about 2 minutes, or until toasty and the cheese has melted. The paninis are shown on page 198 with rustic whole-grain cranberry bread.

Some conventional black bean dips can be a little heavy in both calories and taste. Sometimes when serving veggies and crackers, the dip covers up the various vegetable flavors. This black bean dip is subtle but has a little zip to it. Just get your food processor out and you can whip up a batch in no time. You don't want to sabotage the good effort of serving more vegetables with an unhealthy dip. Every ingredient here is beneficial for you, and tastes great, too! This dip is smooth and easy to scoop with veggies, chips, and more. This makes one medium bowl of dip to share.

Light Black Bean Dip

DIRECTIONS:

Place all the ingredients except the chia and hot sauce into the food processor. Purée to a smooth mixture. Add the chia and a dash of hot sauce. Taste and adjust the amount of hot sauce to your liking. Please keep in mind that flavors intensify with time. If you will be chilling the dip in the fridge until it is needed, you may want to make the final adjustments just before you serve so it doesn't get too hot.

½ can rinsed black beans

½ cup low-fat cottage cheese

3 tablespoons white onion chopped

1 stalk celery cut into pieces

½ inch small piece of de-seeded jalapeño pepper

1 or 2 cloves garlic

1½ teaspoon ground cumin

1 teaspoon ground coriander

1 teaspoon dry chia

1–3 dashes (if you dare) hot sauce

This very easy microwave dip can be made ahead of time and then just warmed up right before your guests arrive. It's a great solution if you know you'll be busy once the party starts. It also works quite well for leftovers. If you can open a frozen box of chopped spinach, you are half way there! This is a thick and hearty dip. This makes one medium bowl of dip to share.

Warm Chicken and Spinach Dip

DIRECTIONS:

If you will be using store bought rotisserie chicken, shred about one cup. If you will be using an uncooked chicken breast, cut the breast into large chunks and place in a low-sided baking dish.

Cover and microwave for 2 minutes on high and then turn over and rotate the pieces. Cook another minute or two so that no pink is showing. When cooled slightly, then you may start the shredding process.

Microwave the spinach by placing the frozen brick of spinach in a covered dish following packaging instructions. Cook and drain spinach using a fork to squeeze out the water. In the same casserole dish add the chicken, onion, cream cheese, Swiss cheese, yogurt, chia gel, red pepper flakes, and nutmeg. Stir to combine. Warm the dip for 2–3 minutes on half power. Or this dip can be held in the refrigerator until it should be warmed for your party.

1 10-oz package of frozen chopped spinach

about 1 chicken breast shredded

2 tablespoons onion

3 oz. cream cheese

½ cup shredded Swiss cheese

2 tablespoon plain yogurt

2 tablespoons chia gel

¼ teaspoons nutmeg

1 small sweet red pepper, de-seeded and chopped

1 pinch red pepper flakes

Hummus is a spicy, healthy Mediterranean treat. This blend of beans and spices makes a great dip, spread, or topping. However, if you have discovered the great taste of hummus, you have probably also discovered that it is expensive! Store-bought hummus can be up to $6 for a small plastic tub. It tastes so fantastic that those little tubs don't last long—even for one person. Making your own hummus is a fantastic way to save. This makes about one cup of hummus.

Easy Chia Lemon Hummus

DIRECTIONS:

If you have a food processor, mini chopper, or even a blender, this can literally be made in minutes. First, purée the chickpeas until smooth. Then, add all the other ingredients and purée again until smooth. Your hummus is now complete and ready to be spread on pitas, tortillas, crackers, to be used as a vegetable or chip dip, and even to replace mayo in sandwiches. It can't get any easier than that!

1 can chickpeas/garbanzo beans (rinse and drained)
2 cloves garlic
2 tablespoons lemon juice
2 tablespoons olive oil
1 teaspoon lemon zest
2 tablespoons gelled chia seeds
¼ teaspoon chili powder

How is this hummus recipe good for you? All hummus is made with chickpeas or garbanzo beans. Beans, in general, are rich in plant protein and fiber. Garbanzos are no exception, and they also have some of the essential amino acids. These are substances your body needs, but cannot make on its own. (Tyrosine, tryptophan, and phenylalanine are three you'll find.) The protein and fiber in chickpeas ensure that they are digested slowly. Hummus has a low glycemic index, meaning it won't raise blood sugar rapidly when eaten. This helps provide you with steady energy. Of course, you'll find vitamin C in the lemon juice, but did you know you'll also be getting the trace minerals copper, manganese, molybdenum, and iron? Each of those minerals in tiny amounts can help you with everything from detoxifying the body of sulfites to helping with heart health.

You can get a tasty boost of fiber with these little squares while simultaneously satisfying your chocolate craving! These are not brownies, and they're not meant to be eaten in a big slice—just a little nibble as an afternoon snack or an after dinner treat. They are fruity, chocolaty, and a little bit mocha. This hearty and chewy little snack could just be a *preventative* measure for you. Though beware, there is sugar in this recipe, so don't over-indulge. Makes one 8 x 8 pan of nibbles.

Chocolate Prune Nibbles

DIRECTIONS:

This prepares quickly, so preheat the oven to 350 and spray your 8 x 8 square baking dish with cooking spray.

Put 7–8 prunes in your mini chopper, food processor, or blender with 2 tablespoons of hot water. Chop until smooth. If need be, add more water ½ teaspoon at a time. Paste will be thick.

In the microwave, melt the chocolate squares for about 40 seconds.

In a bowl, place the melted chocolate, prune purée, eggs, sugar, and vanilla. Beat until blended. Stir in the chia gel. Mix in the flour, salt, instant coffee, and baking powder. Stir to combine.

Spread into the prepared baking pan. Bake for about 30 minutes or until the toothpick comes out clean.

Cool completely before cutting into very small, bite-size squares.

4 1-oz squares unsweetened chocolate
¼ cup of prune purée
½ cup flour
¾ cup sugar
2 eggs
2 tablespoon chia gel
1 teaspoon baking powder
dash salt
1 tablespoon instant coffee OR espresso instant coffee
1 teaspoon vanilla

Dried Plums and Bone Health? Recently, studies have been done on how to help maintain strong bones throughout life. One fruit comes out ahead of the pack in lots of studies: the dried plum. Apparently, dried plums have specific polyphenols in them that slow the bone break-down process to give new bone time to grow. Dr. Bahram Arjmandi says: "Over my career, I have tested numerous fruits, and none of them come anywhere close to having the effect on bone density that the dried plum has." Dr. Bahram Arjmandi is the Director of the Center for Advancing Exercise and Nutrition Research on Aging and the head of research at Florida State University (FSU).[1]

[1] http://news.fsu.edu/More-FSU-News/News-Archive/2011/August/No-bones-about-it-Eating-dried-plums-helps-prevent-fractures-and-osteoporosis

A popsicle as a healthy snack? Absolutely, when they're made with fruit like these are! Popsicles are a super snack because you can make them all in about ten minutes, then just grab one from the freezer whenever you're craving something a little sweet. The banana fudge pop is so healthy you can even have it for breakfast.

The secret of these pops' texture and flavor is in the banana. A banana won't crystallize into an icy mess like most fruits do when frozen. It has a softer, more appealing creamy texture. If you mix in just a little banana with the fruits of your choice, it prevents them from becoming icy, while not making the whole thing taste like a banana.

These popsicles are pure fruit, with no added sugar. Popsicles are fun to eat, colorful, and appealing for kids. Instead of a bag of chips after school, why not try a chia pop? The chia here helps curb hunger so you can easily make it to the next meal. The number of popsicles you get out of each recipe will depend on the size of your molds.

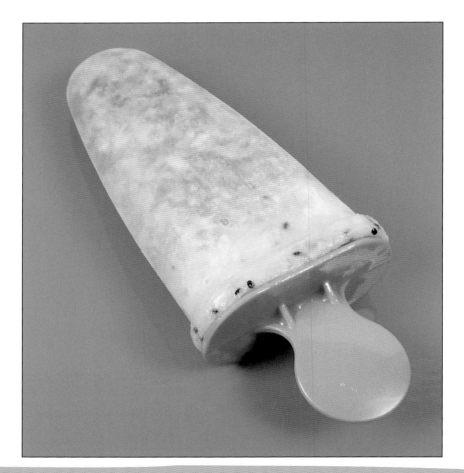

Chia Watermelon Slice Popsicle

These are cute and fun! It's simple to make each pop look like a watermelon slice. If you want to make a dessert version, you can add mini chocolate chips for the "watermelon seeds." Did you know that kiwi seeds are good for you? Make sure to just remove the tough core of the kiwi, but don't discard the little black seeds.

Peel and core the kiwi, then purée the banana and kiwi mixture in the food processor. Taste-test the mixture to see how tart the kiwi is. Kiwis are grown in various countries throughout the year, and some can be sweeter than others. If desired, add the ¼ teaspoon stevia, and mix again to sweeten.

Top off the molds for the last ¼ with the kiwi mixture, place in your popsicle handles, and you're ready to freeze.

For watermelon portion:
½ medium banana
1 cup watermelon cubes
1 teaspoon dry chia seeds

For green "rind" portion:
¼ or ½ of a medium banana
1 kiwi
¼ teaspoon stevia (if desired)

{ The kiwi is a very healthy fruit! It has more vitamin C than an equal amount of orange, as much potassium as a banana, and healthy fiber, too! Kiwi seeds have alpha-linolenic acid and vitamins C and E. }

This popsicle is so incredibly tasty, no one will believe how healthy it is. It looks and feels like a fudge bar, but has only four ingredients, each one of which is excellent for your health. Be sure to use pure, raw, unsweetened and non-dutch-processed cocoa. It packs in the most antioxidants and flavonols for health. The banana is so rich in natural fruit sugars that you won't need any added sweeteners.

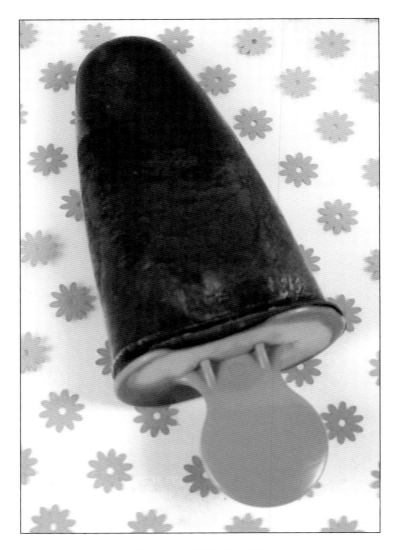

Chocolate Banana Fudgies

DIRECTIONS:

Simply purée ingredients in a food processor, blender, or mini chopper until smooth. Pour into your popsicle molds, freeze, and you're ready to go.

1 large banana (bright yellow/no spots works best)

1 ½ tablespoons unsweetened cocoa powder

1 teaspoon dry chia

3–4 tablespoons unsweetened rice OR almond milk

{ If you want to add variety, you can make a tasty peanut butter version:
Add 1 tablespoon natural unsweetened peanut butter and 1 tablespoon extra milk of your choice. }

Raspberries are a sweet-tart summer treat. Fortunately, they're also available less inexpensively as a frozen fruit. For these pops, the frozen raspberries are a healthy, bright, and eye-opening addition. The watermelon keeps these from being a little too tart. The half of a banana ensures that you get the light creaminess without it tasting like a banana pop.

Raspberry Watermelon Popsicle

DIRECTIONS:

Simply purée ingredients in a food processor, blender, or mini chopper until smooth. Pour into your popsicle molds, freeze, and you're ready to go.

½ regular size banana (yellow, without spots works best)

¼ cup frozen raspberries

¾ cup watermelon cubes

1 teaspoon dry chia

Chia Beverages

You can make almost anything into a chia beverage by simply adding chia gel and stirring it around. Since the chia was already gelled in water, you don't have to think about the acidity of orange juice not allowing dry seeds to gel. Add chia to fruit juices, smoothies, shakes, teas, sports drinks, or just about anything you can think of! You should know that it will take fizz out of carbonated drinks, though.

With the abundance of different unsweetened teas on the market, you won't be at a loss for flavors you enjoy. Some of the fruited teas don't even taste like "tea" at all, so if you don't like tea you might want to give flavors like natural raspberry or natural blueberry a try. These flavors appeal to kids, as well. Want to "juice up" your tea with extra taste? Add a teaspoon of frozen fruit juice concentrate.

Want a sweeter tea? Consider stevia or xylitol. They're plant-based (stevia is a leaf, xylitol is a bark) natural sweeteners that the body does not treat as sugars. They taste sweet, but that is all. Artificial sweeteners like aspartame have actually been studied to increase hunger in certain people. They can also cause side effects or allergic reactions. Stevia is inexpensive and readily available in the supermarket. Just a little will do! Sweetening teas naturally with stevia or agave nectar (or even honey) may tempt kids away from soft drinks with their high fructose corn syrup.

You can brew tea fresh by the cup, or brew it at night and have a pitcher in the fridge, ready to grab at any time. When you prepare easy foods or drinks ahead of time, it reduces the excuses later on.

If you have a favorite drink mix or instant powdered drink mix (a "to-go package") that's meant to be used with a water bottle, chia is great here, too. Just flavor according to package directions, then add your chia, gelled or dry. Shake up the bottle to combine, and you're ready to enjoy.

Chia Fresca

1 cup cold water

2 teaspoons lime juice

1 tablespoon chia gel

stevia, to taste

The drink that started it all! Ancient native people of Mexico made this refreshing drink on hot summer days. They used cold water, sugar cane juice, lime, and chia. The vitamins in the lime juice as well as the nutrients in the chia seeds helped them stay hydrated. As the soluble fiber on the outside of the chia seed is removed by the intestines, it helps hydrate the colon. With this easy recipe, you can enjoy this ancient treat!

Makes one serving of chia fresca.

DIRECTIONS:

Simply stir all ingredients together and drink right away, adding ice cubes if you want.

Green Tea With Mint, Lemon, and Chia

4 green tea bags

juice of half a lemon

1 (or more) tablespoons chia gel

2–3 mint leaves per serving

Really want to knock out hunger? Go for this tea! Green tea has polyphenols that boost leptin, the hormone that silences hunger. Mint is a natural appetite suppressant too, so when both of these get together with chia, it's a powerful force against hunger. A recent study showed people who drink minted green tea (about 2–3 cups per day) consumed 2,800 calories less in a week than the control group who had no tea at all. (And that was without chia!) Be sure to add fresh mint for the best possible taste.

Makes 2 quarts.

DIRECTIONS:

Brew the tea and remove the tea bags once steeped. Cool the tea, and once it is room temperature, add the chia gel and lemon juice. Sweeten to taste with stevia or your choice of natural sweetener. When you're ready to serve, add 2–3 mint leaves per cup. For best results, eat the leaves, too.

Chia concentrate beverages are packed with health and nutrition for the chia lover. However, they do not have the consistency of an ordinary drink. Since the chia is evenly distributed throughout the entire beverage, it has a thicker texture and more powerful fruit flavor. You may have seen bottles of chia drinks like this in trendy supermarkets. Did you know you can create your own at home for a fraction of the cost?

This small recipe makes a quick shot of chia concentrate.

Chia Concentrate Beverages

DIRECTIONS:

Stir together to combine and melt the concentrate. Make sure you use 100 percent fruit juice concentrate, as some frozen or even bottled juices can have added high fructose corn syrup, colors, or artificial flavorings. You don't want to sabotage your good efforts!

1 tablespoon of your favorite juice concentrate

3 tablespoons water

3 tablespoons chia gel

Fruited Chia Teas

To make the fruited chia teas shown here (peach and raspberry) simply brew the tea according to package directions, cool, and stir in your chia gel and stevia.

Hot Chia Beverages

You can use chia in your hot beverages, too. Stirring in a teaspoon or tablespoon of already gelled chia will work great. The coffee shown here has hot frothed almond milk for a cappuccino flavor.

Index